1,200
Paint Effects
for the Home
Decorator

1,200
Paint Effects
for the
Home
Decorator

Ray Bradshaw

NORTH LIGHT BOOKS
Cincinnati, Ohio

PREVIOUS PAGE Marbling the walls in a mixture of colors produces a traditional, harmonious effect.

A QUARTO BOOK

First published in North America in 1997 by North Light Books, an imprint of F & W Publications, Inc.
1507 Dana Avenue
Cincinnati, Ohio 45207
1-800/289-0963

Copyright © 1997 Quarto Inc.
First paperback edition 2000

ISBN 1-58180-057-6

This book was designed and produced by
Quarto Publishing plc
The Old Brewery
6 Blundell Street
London N7 9BH

Senior editor Sally MacEachern
Text editor Mary Senechal
Designer Jenny Dooge
Swatches Ray Bradshaw
Senior art editor Toni Toma
Picture researcher Zöe Holtermann
Editorial director Pippa Rubinstein
Art director Moira Clinch

Typeset by Central Southern Typesetters, Eastbourne
Manufactured in Singapore
by United Graphics (Pte) Ltd.
Printed in Singapore by
Star Standard Industries (Pte) Ltd.

Contents

From 25 basic colors, 1,200 attractive paint effects can easily be achieved.
The paints that are used are water-based latex (emulsion) with a base coat of water-based vinyl semigloss (silk) latex emulsion.

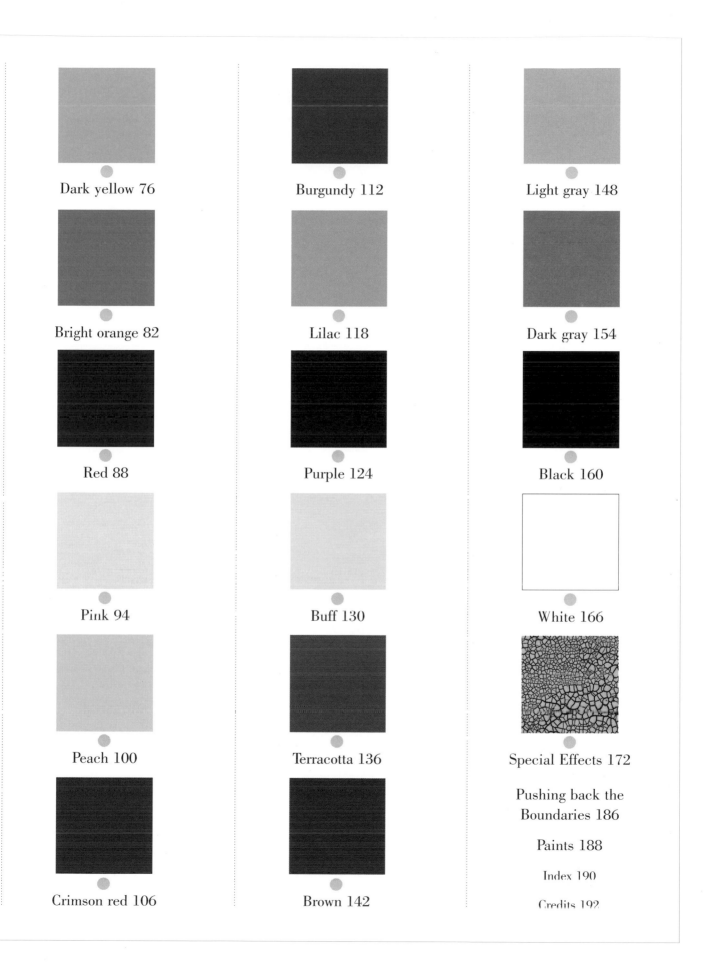

Introduction

Welcome to the infinite world of color: a world of reality, or a world to spark the imagination and conjure memories of a favorite era or place. The choices are endless – and within the reach of even the most inexperienced decorator.

This book is designed to help you create that little bit of magic within your own home. It contains 1,200 different swatches, together with paint and glaze details and "recipes," notes on materials, types of paint, tools, and surfaces. Let us prove to you that success with color, and the use of broken-color work – or paint effects, as they are more generally known – is within your reach.

By viewing the 25 base colors and the effect of each one upon the others, over a range of different paint effects, existing ideas can be strengthened or new ones planted. Brought to fruition, these could enable you to evoke the timelessness of ancient Egypt, with its earthy shades of terracotta and ocher alongside vibrant blues and golds on sandstone walls, or the elegance of the Georgian era with its acid yellows, greens, and pastels. Maybe you prefer a 19th-century atmosphere, using rich burgundies and greens. Perhaps you want to relive an idyllic ocean vacation, with azure skies, rolling seas, and golden sands. Or imagine a romantic starlit sky, seen from a Moorish balcony of marble and sandstone. Yes, washes of color can conjure up that dream.

All of these ideas – and much, much more – can be achieved with the most satisfying results, whether they are

At a glance guide to using the book
The main section of the book, from pages 22–171, is devoted to 25 basic paint colors and each of the colors is shown over 6 pages.

The 25 basic colors are color-coded on each page for easy reference.

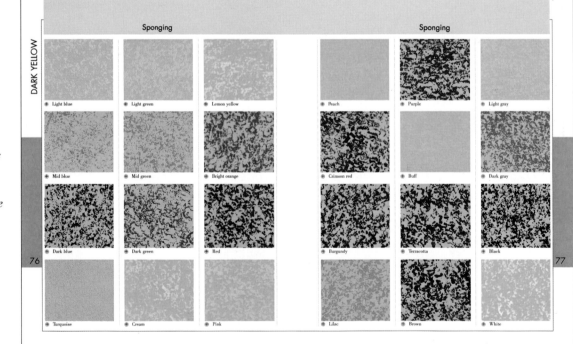

Basic color–pages 1-2
On the first 2 pages, swatches are shown of the basic color used as a base with 24 other colors sponged over the top. These act as "control" pages. If you like a particular color combination, you may decide to use it for the paint techniques on the next pages.

ABOVE The versatility of the sponging technique is demonstrated here where one color is sponged with 24 others.

applied to walls or ceilings, furniture, or window and door frames. With a little understanding and forethought, success and the compliments of friends should be only a short step away. By using this book to its full extent, you can avoid expensive, time-consuming, and sometimes drastic mistakes. By understanding the workings of color and its effects, the manipulation of both oil- and water-based glazes, and where and when to use them, and by knowing how to treat, prepare, and finish different surfaces, complete room transformations are possible for the novice as well as the experienced decorator. By following the advice within these pages, anyone can become confident enough to attempt and carry through those promising ideas.

Remember always that confidence and understanding are the essence of success. Color is highly emotive. Learn by any mistakes, utilize them, or if necessary, paint them out and begin again – your only loss is a coat of paint. Do not be faint-hearted. You will – and should – show your personality through your efforts. You will be surprised at what you can achieve. Be positive, and be creative – for yourself and your family. Feel happy, and remember: it is your home, and your doing; follow your initial impulses, and go for it!

Use this book as a guide on which to draw to create that fantasy, that mood or that atmosphere from which you will gain glorious hours of enjoyment.

USING THIS BOOK

The purpose of this book is to show the home decorator how to accomplish 1,200 stunning paint effects by using a wide spectrum of colors with a variety of techniques. At-a-glance swatches show the home interior designer the effects that can be achieved by using particular techniques and combining colors. Twenty five standard colors are used for the techniques. Each color is mixed with each of the other 24 colors using a sponging technique, then each color is used with one, two or three other colors to demonstrate dragging, spattering, stippling and combing. Each color is combined with either one, two or three other colors and color washed, stenciled, frottaged and rag rolled. Special effects include tortoiseshell finish, malachite, lapis lazuli, verdigris and gilding.

Simply look through the swatches, choose a paint effect and look up the relevant technique. Before starting, check the section on surfaces, preparation and materials to find out how to achieve a professional finish.

Basic color–pages 3-4

RIGHT Four very different and effective paint techniques, using the same base color, are shown here: dragging, spattering, stippling and combing.

Basic color– pages 5-6

RIGHT Color washing, stencilling, frottage and rag rolling are the colorful techniques demonstrated here. All four techniques use the same base color.

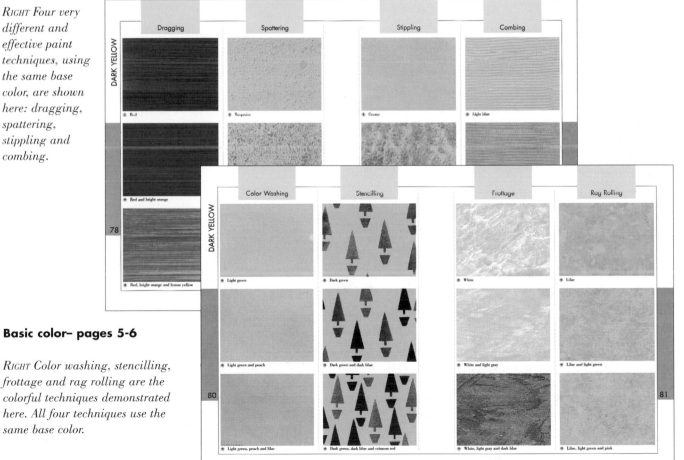

7

Materials:
Paints, Glazes, and Tints

Most of the 1,200 color swatches in this book use water-based latex (emulsion) paints and glazes over a water-based vinyl semigloss (silk) latex (emulsion) base coat. This allows the convenience of working and cleaning up with water, instead of the more toxic and messier turpentine or mineral spirits (white spirit) associated with oil-based products. However, each material has its merits and specific applications, which are explained here, and as you proceed through the book.

Latex (emulsion) paint

Latex (emulsion) is a water-based paint produced in a pouring consistency, or in a gel-like form known as solid latex (emulsion). It comes in four finishes: flat, satin (or eggshell), semi-gloss, gloss (vinyl matte, vinyl soft sheen, vinyl silk, gloss). Flat latex (emulsion) can be applied using a decorating brush or roller, and gives good coverage without sheen on almost any surface. Satin (vinyl soft sheen) provides excellent coverage, with either brush or roller, on most surfaces, drying to a wipeable, subtle sheen. Vinyl semi-gloss (also applied with brush or roller) supplies even color with a more pronounced semi-sheen, once again on most surfaces. The addition of water will "thin," or dilute, the paint to varying consistencies for broken-color work. Approximately 1 part paint to 6 parts water gives a good starting point for color washing. The more water that you add, the more transparent the color will become, and the more subtle your wash will be,

BELOW The gray marble effect on the walls is the ideal backdrop for vibrant colored pictures and furnishings. The standard lamp and cushions stand out from the gray wall.

allowing you to achieve either cloudy or ethereal effects.

Latex (emulsion) is easily tinted with water-based acrylics, universal stainers, and powder pigments. It is relatively inexpensive, and dries in up to 4 hours. It produces a waterproof finish, but may need protection in areas prone to wear and tear, such as kitchens, bathrooms, and playrooms, because dirt and scuff marks are not easily wiped away. It is advised for interior use only. Dry latex (emulsion) can be softened and removed with denatured alcohol (methylated spirits). It has a medium toxicity value (see p.17), and is composed of pigment combined with synthetic resins and/or a polyvinyl acetate binder pigment extender and a flat solvent.

Milk (casein) paints

These water-based paints are carried by specialty stores, and are primarily used on walls and furniture. They are excellent for re-creating traditional and distressed paint finishes. They provide a very flat finish on porous surfaces, where adhesion is at its best. They can be tinted with artists' acrylics or powder pigments; gouache can also be used, but tends to give a weaker effect. The paints are quick-drying but soft, and can easily rub off and scuff if not protected by a sealant (see p.10). They can be lightly polished with waxes for particular "antique" effects. Milk paints are generally for indoor use. They have a medium toxicity value (see p.17), and consist of a pigment in water, a binder (such as casein or gelatin), and sometimes an oil for waterproofing.

Eggshell paint

Available as oil- or water-based paints, these dry to a mid sheen, wipeable surface, and are primarily used for woodwork and walls. The oil-based version produces a harder-wearing surface, good for kitchens and other areas of regular family use. It is recommended for use on chair (dado) rails, baseboards (skirting), and other woodwork, such as doors and window frames. It makes an ideal base coat for marbling (see pp.175 and 179) and tortoiseshelling (see p.183), and is excellent for use with oil-based glazes. It can easily be mixed and tinted with artists' oil paints, oil glaze, and universal stainers. The oil-based paint needs an initial coat of primer and undercoat, especially on porous surfaces, and is slow-drying. Fumes are fairly unpleasant, and the paint must be used with adequate ventilation. Thin it with turpentine or mineral spirits (white spirit). The oil-based paint consists of pigments, synthetic drying oils, and synthetic (alkyd) resin, and its toxicity value (see p.17) is high. The water-based (acrylic) eggshell is a less-toxic, and therefore slightly more user-friendly, alternative, but it is slightly less hard-wearing, and less recommended for walls and woodwork. You do not need to undercoat, just prime.

Satin wood paint, which is based on alkyd resin rather than oil, can be used in place of oil-based eggshell. It gives a greater sheen but less coverage.

Water-based base coats

The base coat is the first coat on the surface upon which the broken-color effects are applied. The color swatches in this book were painted onto a base coat of vinyl semigloss (silk) latex (emulsion). (The feature swatches vary according to technical requirements.) A vinyl semigloss (silk) ground enables the paint and glazes to be easily manipulated without affecting the base coat in any adverse way. A vinyl flat latex (emulsion) or milk paint would be a more absorbent base coat – comparable to watercolor paper – and would produce a harsher effect. Such a base coat might also drag and dissolve if you are not careful. If your base coat is an existing vinyl flat or milk, seal it before applying a paint technique, with a water-based acrylic varnish, which comes in flat or satin finishes.

Direct

These drying and coverage times are manufacturers' guidelines, and can vary according to surface absorbency and atmospheric conditions, such as temperature and humidity.

Product			Coverage	Drying time
primer	18 sq yd/quart	15 sq m/liter		16–24 h
oil-based u/coat	18 sq yd/quart	15 sq m/liter		16–24 h
water-based u/coat	18–20 sq yd/quart	15–17 sq m/liter		2–6 h
oil-based eggshell	18–20 sq yd/quart	15–17 sq m/liter		16–24 h
water-based eggshell	18 sq yd/quart	15 sq m/liter		4–6 h
satinwood (alkyd resin-based)	19 sq yd/quart	16 sq m/liter		16–24 h
vinyl semigloss latex (emulsion)	16½–19 sq yd/quart	14–16 sq m/liter		2–4 h
vinyl satin latex (emulsion)	16½–19 sq yd/quart	14–16 sq m/liter		2–6 h
vinyl flat latex (emulsion)	16½–19 sq yd/quart	14–16 sq m/liter		2–4 h
milk paint	15½ sq yd/quart	13 sq m/liter		1–4 h
oil-based glaze	35 sq yd/quart	30 sq m/liter		7–12 h
water-based glaze	18–24 sq yd/quart	15–20 sq m/liter		2–12 h
oil-based varnish	18 sq yd/quart	15 sq m/liter		6–24 h
water-based varnish	18–24 sq yd/quart	15–20 sq m/liter		15 mins–1 h

ABOVE This elegant black and white bathroom has been given a dramatic marbled finish.

Oil-based or alkyd base coats

Hard-wearing oil-based or alkyd paints are the recommended choice for woodwork and for kitchen cupboards and furniture. They form an excellent base coat for techniques such as marbling (see pp.175 and 179) and wood graining (see p.178), and they are ideal for oil-based glaze work.

Oil-based glazes

Transparent oil glazes make paint more translucent, and extend its working time for up to 30 minutes. Drying can take from 6 to 24 hours, depending on the prevailing atmospheric conditions and the room temperature. The glazes are used in many techniques, notably on furniture, kitchen and bathroom cabinets, and wood. The glazes consist of boiled linseed oil, along with turpentine, liquid driers, and whiting (powdered chalk). They can be tinted with universal stainers, artists' oil colors, and with oil-based paints, such as eggshell. The disadvantages of oil glazes are that they tend to yellow when they are exposed to sunlight, and they need protection, with one or two coats of oil varnish, because they dry to a soft finish. Ready-mixed oil glazes are available from specialist suppliers, and provided you ensure that you follow the manufacturer's instructions, they can save you a lot of time. However, you can also make your own glazes (see the recipe on page 16), to obtain the exact shade and the quantity that you require.

Oil-based colors and tints

Artist's oil colors, used for mixing and tinting, are composed of pigment combined with linseed oil and a drying oil. They are diluted with turpentine or mineral spirits (white spirit), and are slow-drying. Pigments derived from precious and semiprecious stones, such as lapis lazuli, can make some of the tubes expensive, but the effects are well worth it. But nowadays alternatives are made more cheaply from aniline dyes. The colors are slightly translucent and can be mixed with oil glaze for broken-color work, such as rag rolling (see p.20) and dragging (see p.18). Blended with oil-based varnishes (see below) or furniture wax, they can create antiquing or color effects. They are also good for tinting when mixed with gloss and eggshell paint.

Water-based or acrylic glazes and colors

These are very versatile in use and have recently become extremely popular. They are available straight off-the-shelf in good home-decorating stores. Because of their water base, they are much easier and cleaner to use than their oil-based counterparts. They also dry to a soft finish, and must be fixed with a sealant, such as acrylic varnish. They can be tinted with artists' colors, acrylic with latex (emulsion) paint, or with universal stainers and powder pigments. Like oil-based glazes, they make the paint more translucent, and more manageable by extending its working time to about 30 minutes. They dry in 2 to 6 hours. The ideal base for use with them would be vinyl semigloss, or milk paint fixed with a sealant. These glazes also work very well over water-based eggshell paints.

Oil-based varnishes

Copal varnish, polyurethane varnish, marine (yacht) varnish, and spar (carriage) varnish are recommended for good strong protection of all kinds of painted surfaces. They can be mixed with oil-based artists' tube colors, universal stainers, powder pigments, or oil glaze to obtain wonderful antique or tinted finishes. If you apply several coats, sanding between layers, you can achieve a true mirror finish. Drawbacks are that the varnishes are slow-drying; they tend to be yellowish in color; and the polyurethanes can be slightly brittle. Non-yellowing versions of oil-based varnishes are available from specialist stores. These are recommended since you will not want your final effect to yellow unless you want an aged look. Oil-based varnishes contain natural oils and resins, and drying oils in a solvent base of turpentine or mineral spirits (denatured alcohol). Their toxicity value is very high, and they must be used within an adequately ventilated area.

Acrylic or water-based varnishes

These are often preferred, as they have a lower toxicity value, and enable tools and brushes to be cleaned thoroughly with just warm soapy water. They are quick-drying, easy to use, and they can be tinted with universal stainers, powder pigments, and water-based acrylic paints. Acrylic varnish is non-yellowing, heat- and water-resistant, and comes in matte (flat), satin, or gloss finishes.

Brushes and Other Equipment

The most important items of equipment for paint techniques are brushes. There is nothing more frustrating than constantly removing stray bristles from your paintwork. Varnishes and other finishes also need good brushes to achieve a fine, glassy finish on all surfaces. Use the best quality tools that you can. That need not necessarily mean the most expensive, because there are efficient and more moderately priced alternatives available which will produce an equally good result. Synthetic brushes are generally used for oil or water based paints and natural bristle brushes are preferable for oil or alkyd paints.

Standard paint brushes

For priming, undercoating, base coats, and work with oil-based paints, choose a decorator's brush with firm bristles. For water-based latex (emulsion) and glazes, use a more flexible bristle or synthetic brush. The size should suit the job: for example, a 3–4 in (7.5–10 cm) brush for larger areas; and a ½–1 in (1.3–2.5 cm) brush for more intricate work. But more important is to use the size that you find most comfortable – some people feel that a size of 3 in (7.5 cm) or less gives them maximum control in most situations.

Dragging and flogging brushes

The brushes for dragging and flogging (see below) are always long-bristled and flat, to create the subtle effect of fine lines when they are pulled through a glaze. They come in a wide range of sizes.

Standard decorators' brushes

Flogger

Dusting brushes

A dusting brush is the ideal tool for removing small particles from a sanded surface. It is also a viable and less expensive alternative to the badger-hair brush that is used for marbling (see pp.175 and 179) and softening, and in color washing and wood graining.

Lily-bristle dusting brush

Fitches

Fitch brushes of varying sizes and shapes are usually made of hog bristle. They are ideally suited to small-scale effects, such as marbling (see pp.175 and 179), line work, and spattering (p.18) – although an efficient alternative for spattering is the humble toothbrush. They are excellent for detailed work and can be used with both water and oil based paints

Stencil brushes

Brushes for stenciling must have short bristles to limit the amount of paint taken up. They can be round, flat, or domed. Sizes vary from ¼ to 2 in (0.6 to 5 cm) to match the cut-out area and the intricacies of the stencil design. A domed brush with softer bristles is the ideal choice when you want subtle, shaded effects, but a ½ in (1.3 cm) round brush will suit most, if not all, projects.

Stippling brushes

Round, rectangular, or square brushes for stippling (see p.19) are carried by specialist stores, in sizes from ½ to 2 in (1.3 to 5 cm). A large square brush will suit most jobs. Or you could use a good-quality flat-ended or trimmed paint brush. Pads with rubber bristles offer an inexpensive substitute when you want a more open effect.

Selection of round and flat fitches

Varnishing brushes

Special varnishing brushes are useful for large surfaces, because they hold more liquid. In other situations, a good-quality unused paint brush is suitable.

Color washing tools

Color washing is a much-loved effect that can be achieved with a variety of tools or brushes, depending upon the final look you are after. These include sponges (natural or synthetic), lint-free rags, and softening brushes, such as the dusting brush and a 3–6 in (7.5–15 cm) paint brush with flexible bristles.

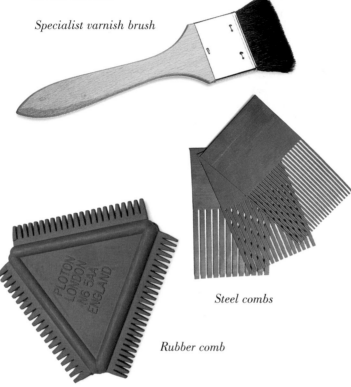

Specialist varnish brush

Steel combs

Rubber comb

Combs

Our combing effects were produced by a triangular rubber comb with three different tooth sizes. A rubber comb is more flexible and therefore easier to control than its metal counterparts. You can also make your own comb from a sturdy piece of cardboard, which will enable you to vary the size of the teeth and spacing to create a wide range of patterns.

Graining rollers

Paint tray and roller in sleeve

Rockers

A rocker (also known as a heart grainer) is used for simple wood graining (see p.178). Generally made of firm rubber, it has a curved surface inscribed with a series of raised concentric circles. It is passed through a glaze while being rocked back and forth to create the appearance of grained wood. Easy to use, it can produce striking effects.

Garnet paper

This is a fine abrasive paper that resists clogging to a greater extent than regular sandpaper.

Lint-free cloth

This term applies to a cloth bought from a paint supplier used for applying or wiping effects that does not shed its fibers. Cotton and silk are ideal. Old T-shirts are excellent. Wash your cloths before use to remove any lint or excess fluff.

Paint rollers

Available in foam or lambswool, rollers are excellent for applying paint to large flat areas, such as walls and ceilings. They eliminate brushstrokes, giving a good, even finish. A problem is that rollers tend to spray droplets of paint onto surrounding areas, so protection is needed for nearby floors or furniture. Special rollers are available for effects such as ragging, lining, and texturing.

Solvents

Solvents are usually the basic constituent of the paint or glaze, and are used for thinning the product and cleaning tools and brushes. They can be water, turpentine, mineral spirits (white spirit), or denatured alcohol (methylated spirits), and each has its own specific applications.

Water is the solvent for all water-based paints, varnishes, and glazes.

Turpentine or mineral spirits (white spirit) is for oil-based products.

Denatured alcohol (methylated spirits) is for shellac sanding sealer, enamel varnishes, and knotting (a sealant for wood knots).

Brand-name solvents or thinners serve much the same purpose as the solvent base of a product. They are primarily designed for the rejuvenation of brushes and other equipment: for example, brush restorer or cleaner. Whatever the solvent, always follow all the manufacturer's instructions to the letter.

1 Silicon carbide
2 Glasspaper
3 Garnetpaper

Paper towels

Their absorbency makes these useful for cleaning up mistakes, wiping off excess paint, and mopping up spillages. They are especially good for removing extra paint from bristles when stenciling.

Sandpaper

Sandpaper is available in a variety of grades from 60 (coarse) to 220 (fine). Use it for smoothing surfaces before the application of the undercoat and the base coat, and for distressing layers of paint. Special sanding blocks and pads are available for increased control. Always make sure to sand wood surfaces along, or with, the grain.

Cleaning your brushes

Taking care of your brushes will extend their life and enable you to produce good-quality work.

Water-based paints and varnishes

Remove water-based paints and varnishes by washing the brush thoroughly in warm running water. Include the topmost end toward the ferrule, and work the bristles downward to remove all traces of paint or varnish. Then cleanse the brush with dishwashing detergent in warm water. Rinse thoroughly. Dry carefully with a soft cloth, and store upright, with handle down, to allow moisture to evaporate.

Oil-based paints, varnishes, and glazes

After using oil-based products, wash the brush thoroughly in turpentine, mineral spirits (white spirit), or paint thinner, applying the same technique as for water-based paints. Rinse again in the cleaner, using a little dishwashing detergent. Finally, rinse thoroughly in warm water. Dry with a cloth, smoothing the bristles away from the ferrule, and hang to dry or store.

Paint and varnish removers

Sometimes you may need to remove old paint and varnish by means other than sandpaper or a paint scraper. Water- or solvent-based chemical strippers available from hardware stores and paint suppliers are useful for intricate areas, carving, and stair spindles. Follow all of the manufacturer's instructions and safety advice when using. Shellac and French polish should be stripped off with denatured alcohol (methylated spirits) and steel wool (medium to fine).

Scrapers

A scraper, consisting of a metal blade in a handle, is used to scrape away excess paint and varnish. It is also effective in conjunction with paint and varnish removers, allowing you to peel away the layers of unwanted coating as the stripper works. However, it is a rough-and-ready method of stripping, and should always be followed by sanding.

Sponges

Synthetic sponges are ideal for the addition or removal of glaze in color washing, and for softening edges in cloudy effects. They can also be cut into shapes for simple stamping on flat surfaces. They are readily available and cheap. Natural sponges are used for the decorative effect of sponging (see below). They can be bought from drugstores and decorating suppliers, and are fairly expensive, but they can be purchased by size. The textures vary enormously, and a sponge can become a personalized tool. So when you find one with an effect you like, keep it in good condition.

Marine and synthetic sponges

Steel wool (wire wool)

This comes in grades varying from very fine to coarse, from hardware and decorating stores. Use very fine grades for cutting back varnish and oil finishes, and between paint coats; medium to fine for clearing dirt, wax, and surface paint before repainting; and grades up to coarse, with chemical strippers, for the removal of old paint and varnish. Steel wool is sharp – cut it with shears or scissors.

Tack cloth

This is a piece of cheesecloth impregnated with varnish and linseed oil to make it "tacky," or sticky. It attracts specks of dirt and cleans surfaces of dust and lint. This produces a smooth surface that is ready for paint effects, especially those such as marble and tortoiseshell.

Wet-and-dry sandpaper

As its name implies, this abrasive paper can be used either wet or dry. The use of a lubricant (usually water) helps prevent clogging and maintains the sharpness of the paper. It is ideal for work on metal, and in special effects.

Preparation

As with most things in life, the preparation part of a project tends to be the least popular. We are generally too impatient to see the finished scheme. But it is essential to observe the groundwork requirements for each effect in order to produce good-quality results, and to avoid mistakes that can show up weeks later. Different effects call for different preparation, and not all of it has to be absolutely perfect! Effects such as color washing can look superb when applied over uneven plaster, for example. Color work such as sponging (see p.18) and rag rolling (see p.20) does "cover a multitude of sins": Hairline cracks and uneven areas of wall can be effectively disguised by these techniques, especially when two colors are incorporated.

Surfaces

As a result of modern technology, most, if not all, surfaces can be given a decorative finish. Paint effects are most often applied to walls and woodwork, but you can equally well treat furniture, including kitchen, bathroom, and bedroom cupboards and closets, made from a variety of materials. Effects on small decorative items, such as boxes, candlesticks, vases, plant stands, and picture frames, can be the essential, personal statement that brings an entire scheme together. These objects respond well to some of the specialty finishes – marbling, malachite, wood graining, and tortoiseshelling, for example – shown on the feature swatches (pp.172–185). Nor do we need to neglect the outside of the house: most of the techniques shown here can also be applied to exterior walls, and outdoor furniture, provided you protect them adequately.

Whatever your surface, you need to consider its present condition and the amount of wear and tear it will receive. Is it in a vulnerable position? Will it need frequent cleaning, or is it purely decorative? The answers to such questions will guide you to the type of paint and final protection best suited for the project. A surface likely to suffer from dirt or knocks will benefit from oil-based paint. If water-based paint, such as milk or acrylic, is chosen, it would be advisable to seal the finished effect with one or two coats of varnish – oil-based for maximum protection, or a modern acrylic varnish that is heat- and water-resistant. External surfaces must be safeguarded with at least two coats of oil-based varnish. The table on p.15 provides a convenient guide to the choice and preparation of available surfaces, and their final protection. You will find more information about varnishes on page 10.

Paint, wallpaper, and plaster

The two basic surfaces that you are likely to encounter are plaster and wood, and each has its set of preparation rules. Faced with a plaster wall that is covered in loose paint or wallpaper, think carefully. You could find yourself stripping away many layers of paint or paper, and inadvertently creating additional problems of crumbling plaster and gaping cracks, all of which will need to be filled and sanded. Ask yourself if these layers can just be sanded, primed, and undercoated to achieve the effect you need, or if they must definitely be removed.

It is undoubtedly true that thorough preparation is the surest way to a top-quality finish that will last for years. If this is your choice, or conditions demand it, obtain a wallpaper stripper and spend a weekend carefully removing every layer. Use a good-quality scraper gently, being careful not to gouge out holes in the underlying plaster. When the paper is off, check for holes and cracks, and fill them with a ready-made filler. Allow this to dry overnight, and then give it a good sanding with first a medium-grade and finally a fine-grade sandpaper. The smoothness will depend on the effect you plan to apply. Pay special attention to any areas where light from a window or lamp would accentuate a fault.

If the walls have been replastered, even partially, apply a coat of neutral-colored latex (emulsion) paint thinned half and half with water, to seal them. Then use a 3–4 in (7.5–10 cm) paintbrush or a roller to add one (or, if necessary, two) base coats of your chosen color. Allow the wall to dry between coats. Vinyl semigloss (silk) latex (emulsion) works well over plaster as a base for any of the broken-color effects.

Wood

Wooden furniture and fixtures need thorough preparation, because the surface is likely to show up any flaws quite noticeably. Wood is also the most frequent base for glaze finishes, whose success depends on good preparation. Strip all loose flakes of paint and varnish from previously treated wood, using a suitable ready-made remover (see p.13) in accordance with the manufacturer's instructions. Clean grease from kitchen cupboards by washing them down with a degreasing agent. Rinse thoroughly with clean water. Let surface dry before painting the base coat. Fill cracks and nail holes with wood filler, allow to dry, and sand. After filling, and again after sanding, remove all traces of dust with a soft cloth and dusting brush. An excellent alternative to these is a tack cloth (a cloth permeated with linseed oil). Seal with shellac (knotting), or sanding sealer, and then apply a primer and undercoat before the base coat.

Melamine

This popular surface for bedroom, bathroom, and kitchen furnishings must be carefully prepared; if not, the finishes are likely to peel, or suffer damage from the slightest knock. Remove any surface additives, such as glue, wash down thoroughly with degreasing agent, rinse, and allow to dry. Sand with medium- or fine-grade sandpaper so that the primer can adhere. Prime and undercoat with oil-based products. Allow to dry between coats. Finally, paint on one or two layers of oil-based eggshell and leave to dry. Carry out broken-color work, using either oil-based or

Surfaces: suitability and preparation

surface	suitability for decoration	preparation	undercoat/ base coat	suitable effects	unsuitable effects	protection
walls (textured)	good	remove flaking paint fill cracks sand	undercoat base coat of latex (emulsion)	most paint effects	dragging combing	suitable varnish or sealant
walls (smooth)	excellent	remove flaking paint, wallpaper, etc. fill cracks sand	undercoat base coat of latex (emulsion)	all paint effects		suitable varnish or sealant
woodwork (doors, etc.)	excellent	remove loose paint fill holes sand	prime undercoat base coat of eggshell/ satin wood	all paint effects		suitable varnish or sealant
metal	good	remove grease and rust sand seal with rust sealer	prime undercoat base coat of oil-based paint	all paint effects		suitable varnish or sealant
plastic (non glossy)	average	remove grease sand for tooth	prime undercoat base coat oil-based paint	all paint effects		suitable varnish or sealant
glass ceramics	good	clean with denatured alcohol or glass cleaner and dry	oil-based undercoat base coat of oil-based eggshell	hand painting, stencilling etc.	dragging combing	suitable varnish or sealant
furniture	excellent	remove loose paint and varnish sand	undercoat base coat of latex (emulsion) or eggshell	all paint effects		suitable varnish or sealant
melamine	good	clean with degreasing agent, rinse, sand	prime undercoat base coat of eggshell	all paint effects		oil-based varnish
outdoor (walls, furniture, etc.)	good	remove loose particles, grease, etc.	undercoat base coat of outdoor paint	most paint effects		suitable outdoor varnish

acrylic glazes. After drying, seal thoroughly with two coats of oil-based varnish. This may seem like a lot of work, but for only a fraction of the cost of a brand-new kitchen, bedroom, or bathroom, you can achieve a complete transformation.

Matte plastic can be treated in a similar way, but shiny or gloss plastic, while not impossible, is not recommended for paint effects.

Metal

Completing a scheme may involve painting metal accessories, such as candlesticks, lampbases, and wastebaskets. All paint effects are suitable for these, following adequate preparation. They must be cleaned, de-rusted, primed, and undercoated. Remove any rust by rubbing first with steel wool, and then with emery cloth or wet-and-dry sandpaper. The grades of wool and sandpaper to use will be dependent on the object and its present condition, ranging from coarse for, say, a patio table, to fine for a small lampbase. Allow the object to dry then apply a rust sealer, followed by a primer and an undercoat. Use oil-based or water-based paint for the base coat. Protect the final decoration with a coating of varnish.

Glass and ceramics

Clean glass and ceramics thoroughly with denatured alcohol (methylated spirits), and allow to dry. Apply an oil-based undercoat and a base coat of oil-based eggshell. Use oil-based paints or glazes, or acrylic for your effect, and seal the finished piece with varnish. Subsequent cleaning should be done with a damp cloth only. The best effects for these surfaces are hand painting and stenciling, and there is a special line of cold cure ceramic paints available for these, although the range of colors is not great. These paints have very low toxicity, but are for decorative purposes only, and should not be applied to items such as glassware and crockery which are in everyday use.

Outdoor surfaces

Brick or concrete walls and pavings, outdoor furniture, and plant pots, can be decorated. Use oil-based paints or glazes for furniture and pots, and finish with two or more coats of oil-based varnish, such as spar (carriage) varnish. Allow at least 24 hours between coats. Walls and floors of brick or concrete can be decorated with concrete floor paint, following the manufacturer's instructions. They should not need sealing.

Glazes

A glaze is a transparent layer of color, generally applied over an opaque base coat to create depth and variable intensities of color. You could make a glaze simply by thinning your chosen oil- or water-based paint with its relevant solvent, and applying it over the base coat. However, the addition of neutral glazes extends the working time, so that even a novice decorator can achieve a quality result.

How to make glazes

Ready-made oil- and water-based glazes are available over the counter from good interior decorating supply stores. But making your own glaze can give you an effective product with little or no waste, provided you follow the instructions carefully. Both types of glaze can be made, but the water-based glaze will not be as durable as its store-bought equivalent, which contains stabilizers. The following recipes are suitable for the effects shown in this book. Like ready-made glazes, they will dry to a soft finish, and must be protected with a suitable varnish (see p.10).

Transparent oil glaze

INGREDIENTS
1 part pure turpentine
1 part boiled linseed oil
5% liquid driers (drying agents,
obtainable from decorating or hardware stores)
10% white oil paint flat
Oil color for tinting

METHOD
Whisk all the ingredients together thoroughly, and store in an airtight container. The more driers you add, the shorter the drying time. The more oil or turpentine, the greater the drying time. Tint with oil-based paint, universal stainers, or artist's oil tube colors.

Water-based glaze

INGREDIENTS
PVA- or acrylic-based wallpaper paste
containing antifungicide
Water-based color

METHOD
Use a good-quality PVA- or acrylic-based wallpaper paste that contains an antifungicidal agent. Cheaper alternatives will not give satisfactory results. Tint it with water-based colors, and dilute with water to a thin creamy consistency.

Coloring oil- and water-based glazes

Tinting must be done slowly and carefully because most stainers and colors are intense (see p.8–10) for suitable sources of color). Place a small amount of the tint in a clean container and dilute with a little of the relevant solvent – for example, water for water-based glazes; mineral spirits (white spirit) or turpentine for oil glazes. Mix thoroughly. Add a little more solvent, and mix again to a smooth consistency. Add a little of the glaze you want to color, and again stir well to incorporate any excess tint. Add the mixture to the glaze in a clean container, and mix again. Test on a sample board for color accuracy, and adjust as necessary. You are now ready to begin work.

Testing your planned effect with sample boards before you apply a finish to the main project can eliminate time-consuming mistakes.

Popular and traditional glaze colors

As we all know, people have their own opinions and idiosyncracies, and if everyone liked the same style, we would certainly live in a dull world! Advice can be given about colors, color schemes, and techniques, but the ultimate choice must belong to the individual.

Nevertheless, we are bound to be influenced by factors such as where we live, our national history and culture, and by social and technological change. Over the centuries, fashions of style and color have altered and also returned in modified forms. Even the most dedicated follower of current trends is unlikely to shake off entirely the heritage of the past. But today we are in the privileged position of being able to take our inspiration from virtually any era or part of the world. Whatever our shared influences, we can draw on them to create an environment that expresses our own personality and releases us from slavery to fashion.

In the past, color was largely dependent upon geographical location and the availability of pigments, although style influences traveled along trade routes, and by way of exploration and military expeditions. There was always also an element of experimentation, from prehistoric times, through the alchemy of the 17th and 18th centuries, to modern-day technological research. In the cave paintings of South America and Australasia, the predominant colors were the earth and vegetable pigments: ochers and reds, browns and blacks, along with tinges of greens and yellows. At the end of the 17th and for much of the 18th century, throughout Europe and in North America, colors were subdued, including somewhat dull greens and muted earth colors. As the 18th century progressed, colors lightened with the use of pastel colors, often accentuated with solid, strong hues. The end of the 18th century also brought the revival of a classical style, reminiscent of ancient Greece or

effect	most suitable base coat	alternative base coat	quality of surface	glaze to use	suitable for	final protection	toxicity
					Suitable applications, base coats, and effects for oil-based, and acrylic glazes		
sponging	vinyl semigloss (silk) latex (emulsion)	vinyl flat latex (emulsion) melamine	poor to excellent	acrylic	walls furniture small items	suitable varnish if vulnerable	low
dragging	eggshell	vinyl silk melamine	excellent	oil or acrylic	walls woodwork furniture	suitable varnish	oil glaze high acrylic low
spattering	vinyl semigloss (silk) eggshell	vinyl flat latex (emulsion) melamine	poor to excellent	oil or acrylic	walls furniture small items	suitable varnish	oil glaze high acrylic low
stippling	eggshell	vinyl semigloss (silk) melamine	excellent	oil or acrylic	walls furniture	suitable varnish	oil glaze high acrylic low
combing	eggshell	vinyl semigloss (silk) melamine	excellent	oil or acrylic	walls furniture	suitable varnish	oil glaze high acrylic low
color washing	vinyl semigloss (silk) latex (emulsion)	eggshell melamine	poor to excellent	oil or acrylic	walls small items	suitable varnish	oil glaze high acrylic low
frottage	all base coats		poor to excellent	oil or acrylic	walls furniture	suitable varnish if vulnerable	oil glaze high acrylic low
rag rolling	vinyl semigloss (silk) latex	vinyl flat latex (emulsion)	poor to excellent	oil or acrylic	walls furniture	suitable varnish if	oil glaze high acrylic low

Rome. Color became more vibrant, and the designers more innovative. The 19th century extended the palette with richer and deeper tones of green, burgundy, and blue.

For most of us, the 20th century has brought mood and style changes from all corners of the globe. The United States enjoyed and exported the stylized look of the 1920s and early 1930s, with its vivid greens, blues, and yellows, highlighted with metallic golds and silver, along with black and tones of gray: a look that spoke of dance, fun, and, of course, prohibition. North from the Mediterranean came aesthetic color washes of blues, greens, and terra cottas, and the simplicity of white. From the far reaches of the Pacific to the beautiful islands of the Caribbean came full, vibrant reds, yellows, oranges, and greens. Today the choice is boundless.

Testing the glaze

After choosing and mixing your colors, check out the effect of your glaze on some sample boards. Testing the glaze on the base coat will give you a chance to assess the color as it will finally appear, and to become familiar with the way the glaze works on your intended ground. You can then carry out any necessary fine-tuning of the glaze, the color, or the ground.

Fine-tuning the glaze, color, and ground

To achieve the exact shade you want in a particular glaze or ground color, you may need to spend a little time experimenting. This is easy, provided you follow a few simple rules. Begin with the lighter colors; darkening comes last. Remember to darken with a hint of raw umber, and not with black. Always dissolve a minimal amount of color in the solvent, and add a little at a time to the basic glaze, mixing each addition thoroughly. Test regularly on a sample board of the chosen ground color to ascertain the mutual effect of glaze and base color. Colors also vary when dry so allow your test patch to dry before continuing. Note the quantities you use, and when you achieve the shade you want, mix up enough glaze to finish the job, because mixing and matching later is likely to be impossible.

If the glaze is not easily workable at this stage, add a little more of the clear glaze, and mix thoroughly. If it remains hard to manipulate, stir in some of the relevant solvent, a fraction at a time, until you achieve the fluidity of cream. By patient adherence to this judicious dosing, you will reach the correct color and the most workable consistency.

Correcting mistakes

Unsightly blotches, or an over-dark area can be removed while the glaze is still wet. Wipe off mistakes in an oil-based glaze using a lint-free cloth dampened with turpentine or denatured alcohol (methylated spirits). Apply a little more glaze, and patch up the effect, working fairly quickly. Water-based glazes dry more rapidly, so errors must be removed very quickly. Wipe off the glaze with a water-dampened cloth, apply new glaze, and paint the effect again. If you cannot erase mistakes to your satisfaction, it is not the end of the world — you can always remove as much of the glaze as possible, repaint the base coat, and start over.

Techniques

The techniques described here are simple, and attractive results can be achieved by beginners. The important thing to remember is to employ appropriate techniques, to use the correct equipment, and to carry out the recommended preparations to the surface. Above all, experiment for yourself with color until you produce the effect that you want. There are many suggestions for finishes, but again, try different ones until you achieve something that is pleasing to you.

Sponging

Sponging is a striking effect, enhanced by the use of two or more colors, and is simple to achieve. It is the effect used in this book for the "control" pages of each color. Dip a natural sponge into the glaze, dab it onto a cloth or paper towel to remove the excess, and apply it haphazardly to the ground. Work quickly, and do not press too hard, because this will create blotched areas. Do not turn the sponge while it is in contact with the surface. This would cause smudging, out of keeping with the crisp and natural look. The related effect of sponging off is achieved by painting the ground with the glaze, stippling out (see p.19) the brushstrokes and flaws, and then removing the glaze with a clean sponge. Dab the sponge onto the surface, and remove it quickly. Wash the sponge often to prevent the buildup of glaze.

Dragging

Dragging is an elegant, lined effect that results from passing a long-haired dragging brush through a wet glaze, allowing the base coat to show through. It is an excellent effect for walls, chair (dado) rails, base boards (skirting boards), and door or window frames or furniture and small decorative items. Good preparation is essential, since the brushstrokes will pick up any faults. Paint the glaze over the base coat, using a pliable, suitably sized paint brush. Keep the coat of glaze even by stippling (see p.19), to smooth any joins between regular brushstrokes, and to redistribute denser areas of glaze. Start at the top and drag the brush through the wet glaze, in one clean stroke. Remove excess glaze from the brush with paper towels. Repeat if necessary to even out the glaze.

Spattering

This speckled effect can be used on virtually all surfaces. It is ideal for lampbases, tables, and smaller items of furniture, and for creating the appearance of granite or other stone. Load a stiff-bristled paintbrush, or a toothbrush, with paint, and draw your finger or a knife blade over the bristles to release a spray of fine drops onto the base coat. The size of the specks will depend upon the length of the bristles, the speed of release, and your distance from the surface. The effect can be very subtle depending on the colors used. Two colors that are quite similar will produce a more subdued look, while dissimilar colors will give a lively contrasting appearance. Some extremely dramatic effects can be achieved with spattering.

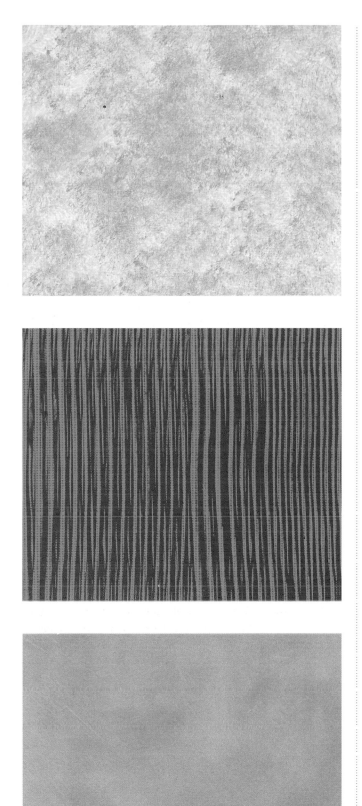

Stippling

Stippling creates a subtle allover effect of depth and simplicity. It is done by pressing a dry stippling brush into the glaze to distribute the brushstrokes into an even pattern. The stiffer the bristles, the more open and stronger the effect will be. Stippling is ideal for use on door panels and tabletops, and for creating even, transparent glaze layers on walls and furniture. The method can be used to eliminate brushstrokes in glazes before applying additional effects, such as dragging and rag rolling, and stippling makes an excellent base for hand painting or stenciling. A well-prepared surface is needed, since stippling can accentuate flaws. Paint the glaze onto the base coat, using a pliable paint brush. Then "pounce" the stippling brush into the glaze, allowing the bristles to act as springs. Aim for a uniform effect without obvious brush lines, and clean the brush regularly. A stippling pad with rubber bristles can be used to produce a bolder, more open stipple.

Combing

You can immediately create a pronounced pattern by passing a comb through a wet glaze. This can be over-combed in different directions and colors when the bottom layer is dry. Varying the width of the comb and the pattern of colors produces lush tartans and plaids (see swatches). Utilizing the comb in wavy patterns can create optical fantasies.

This technique makes a strong statement. It works well on furniture and walls, and is especially effective using different layers of color, allowed to dry between coats. Choose the most suitable comb. Then paint the glaze onto the ground coat, and stipple out (see above) brushstrokes. Place the comb on the wet glaze, and pull it toward you in one clean sweep. Remove excess glaze from the comb with a lint-free cloth, and work the pattern across the base coat. Many-layered effects can be achieved by pulling the comb in different directions, producing wavy lines and straight or circular patterns.

Color washing

Color washing is a charming and versatile effect, mainly for use on walls. Choose the colors carefully, so that each reflects off the one below – sample boards will help. Washes are easy to make, either from paint or from water- or oil-based glazes. Thin paint with its solvent, start with approximately 1 part paint to 6 parts solvent or glaze for water-based paints and glazes. Thin to increase transparency. Paint the glaze randomly onto the base coat, using a soft flexible brush to achieve a cloudy effect, allowing parts of the base to show through. Work over a 1–2 sq yd (1–2 sq m) area, always keeping a wet edge to avoid buildup of color intensity. Soften the brushstroke as you paint, with a softening brush, until the required balance is achieved. More background color can be revealed by removing areas of glaze with a soft household sponge or lint-free cloth before it dries. Or you can increase the effect by working in another color during drying. When the first layer is dry, you can apply another, following the same method.

19

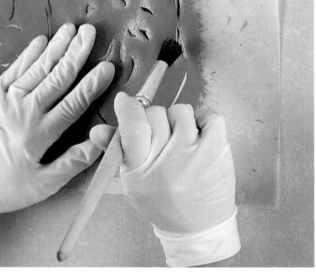

Rag rolling

This is a popular effect, which can be used with one, two, or three colors. this technique will camouflage minor flaws.

There are two methods of rag rolling: ragging on and ragging off. Ragging on is achieved by applying glaze with a cotton, chamois, silk or absorbent kitchen cloth. Each will produce a different appearance. Dip the cloth into the glaze, and remove the excess. Twist the cloth into a loose shape, tucking in the ends to prevent them touching the base coat. Apply the cloth to the base coat, and roll it randomly away from you in all directions. Work from the bottom up to avoid catching your fingers under the cloth. Apply any additional color in the same way, after the previous layer has dried.

Ragging off produces a more pronounced effect. It is achieved by painting the glaze onto the base coat, stippling out (see p.19) the brushstrokes, and rolling a dry rag over the surface to remove glaze.

Stenciling

Stenciling is the art of producing a design by applying paint through a cut-out image. (Glaze is not suitable for stenciling, because it is too thin and would run or bleed.) An effect used since ancient times, and a favorite of the 1930s, it is enjoying a welcome revival. Designs and applications are as varied as imagination and ingenuity will allow.

You can produce myriad patterns from store-bought or homemade stencils, or combine different stencils and broken-color work to create balcony views, walled gardens, or exotic jungles. Stipple (see p.19) or swirl the paint onto your base coat, through the cut-out areas of the stencil, using a stencil brush (see p.11) or a proprietary cellulose stencil sponge.

Create your own patterns for stencils using popular motifs copied from, books, magazines and wrapping paper Always experiment before trying out the stencil on to the item to be decorated.

Frottage

This is a quick and easy way of using a glaze. It can be enhanced with two or three layers of transparent color. It also covers up hairline cracks and imperfections. Have plenty of newspaper nearby, because this is the essence of frottage. Paint your chosen glaze over the base coat liberally and randomly, keeping a wet edge, and stipple out the brushstrokes. Place a sheet of newspaper on top of the wet glaze, and press out with a soft cloth or sponge. Do not worry about achieving a completely smooth surface – slight wrinkles in the paper will enhance the effect. Remove the sheet after pressing, and discard. Continue with a new sheet if necessary to cover the surface. Let the glaze dry slightly. Blend in another color, stipple, add the newsprint, press and remove.

RIGHT A warm ocher is used to stipple the wall, which makes a perfect setting for distressed furniture.

SWATCHES

Sponging

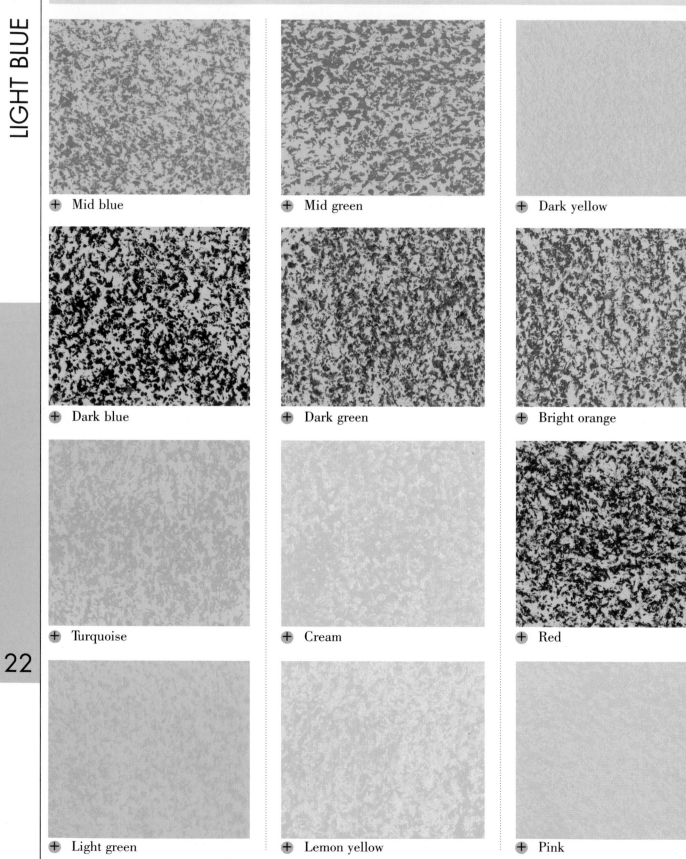

+ Mid blue

+ Mid green

+ Dark yellow

+ Dark blue

+ Dark green

+ Bright orange

+ Turquoise

+ Cream

+ Red

+ Light green

+ Lemon yellow

+ Pink

22

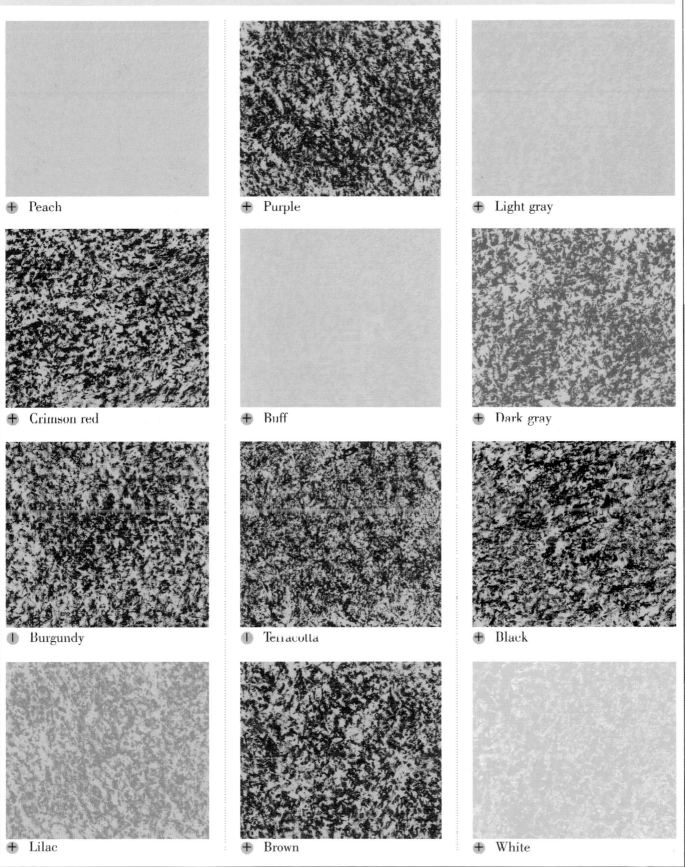

+ Peach

+ Purple

+ Light gray

+ Crimson red

+ Buff

+ Dark gray

I Burgundy

I Terracotta

+ Black

+ Lilac

+ Brown

+ White

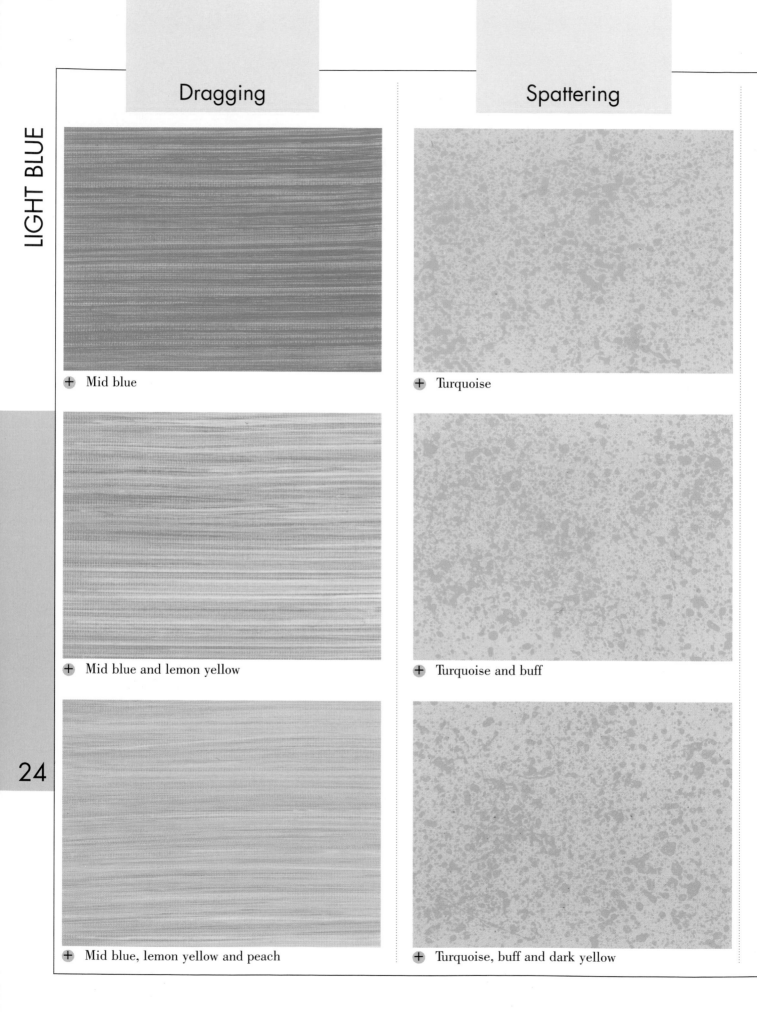

Dragging

Spattering

+ Mid blue

+ Turquoise

+ Mid blue and lemon yellow

+ Turquoise and buff

+ Mid blue, lemon yellow and peach

+ Turquoise, buff and dark yellow

Stippling

Combing

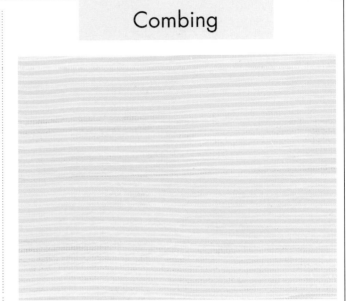

+ Crimson red

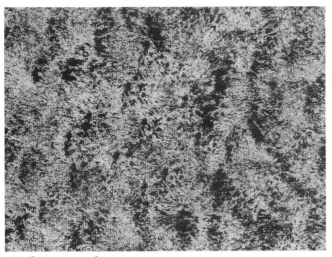

+ Lemon yellow

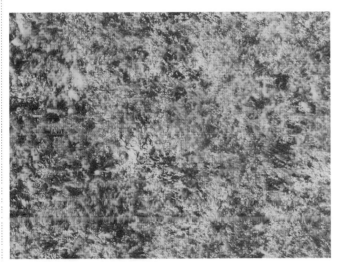

+ Crimson red and buff

+ Lemon yellow and bright orange

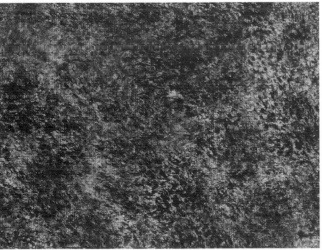

+ Crimson red, buff and burgundy

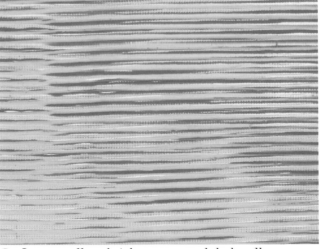

+ Lemon yellow, bright orange and dark yellow

25

Color Washing

Stencilling

 Dark green

+ Lilac

+ Dark green and light gray

+ Lilac and mid blue

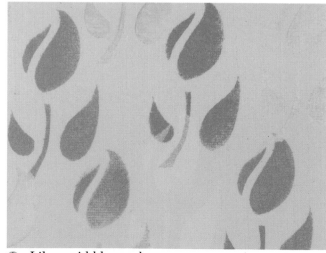

+ Dark green, light gray and dark yellow

+ Lilac, mid blue and cream

Frottage

Rag Rolling

⊕ Light gray

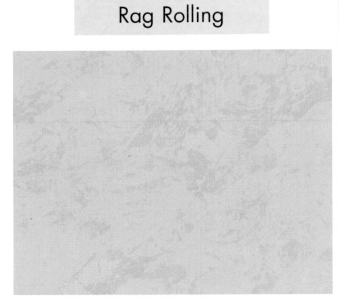

⊕ Light green

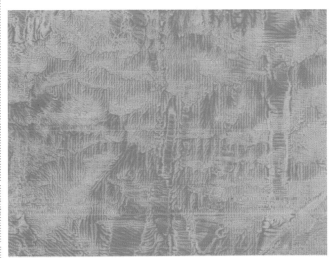

⊕ Light gray and mid blue

⊕ Light green and mid green

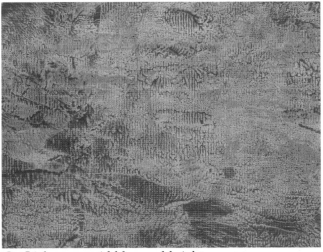

⊕ Light gray, mid blue and bright orange

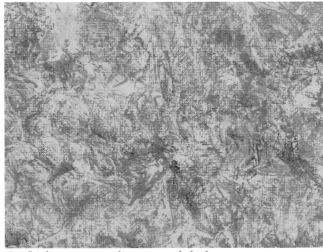

⊕ Light green, mid green and dark green

27

Sponging

⊕ Light Blue

⊕ Mid Green

 ⊕ Dark Yellow

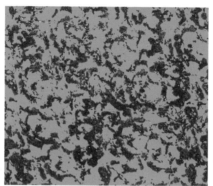

⊕ Dark Blue

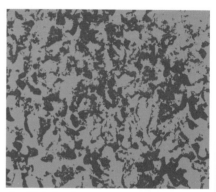

⊕ Dark Green

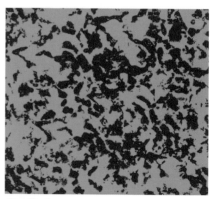

⊕ Bright Orange

⊕ Turquoise

⊕ Cream

⊕ Red

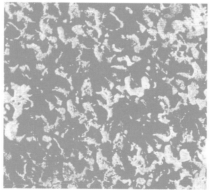

⊕ Light Green

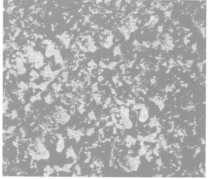

⊕ Lemon Yellow

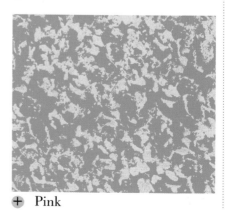

⊕ Pink

+ Peach

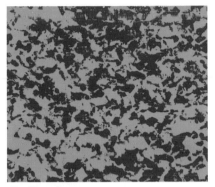

+ Purple

+ Light gray

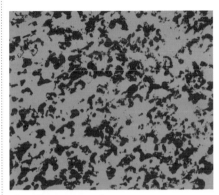

+ Crimson red

+ Buff

+ Dark gray

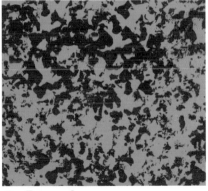

+ Burgundy

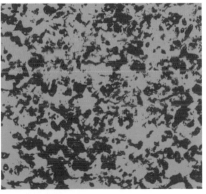

+ Terracotta

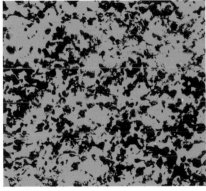

+ Black

+ Lilac

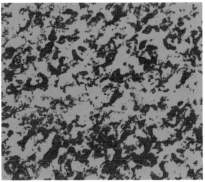

+ Brown

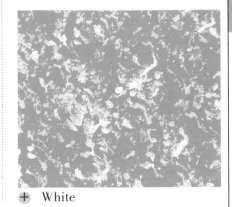

+ White

Dragging

Spattering

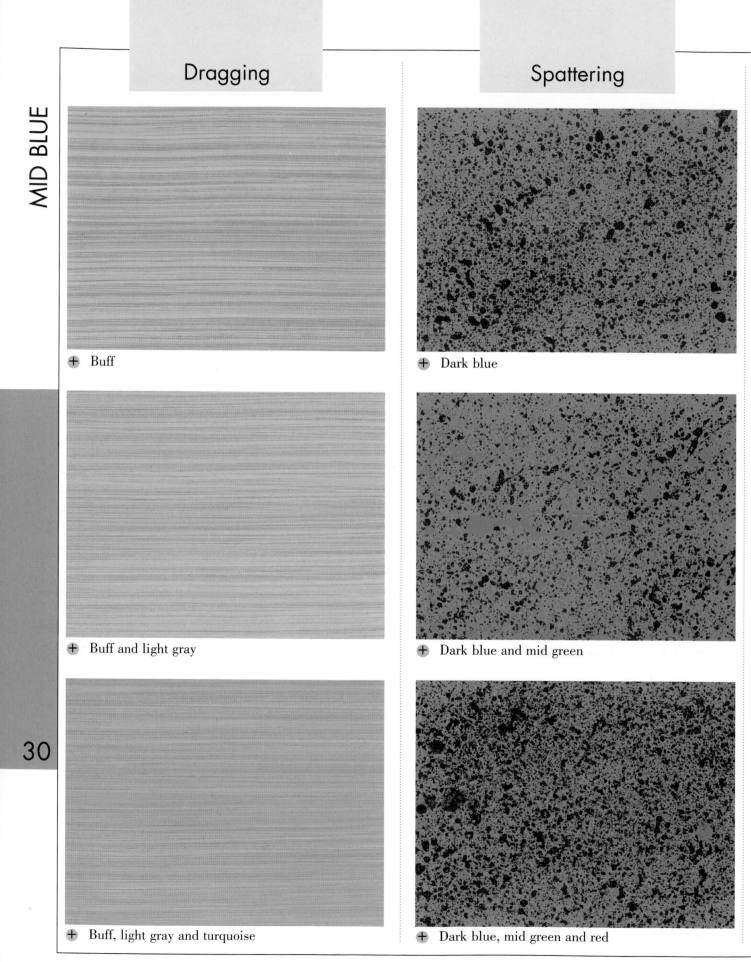

+ Buff

+ Dark blue

+ Buff and light gray

+ Dark blue and mid green

+ Buff, light gray and turquoise

+ Dark blue, mid green and red

Stippling

Combing

+ Dark yellow

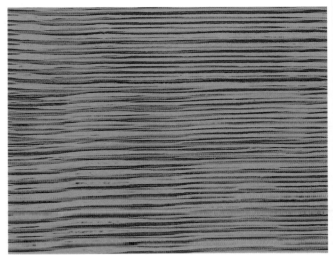

+ Dark blue

+ Dark yellow and lemon yellow

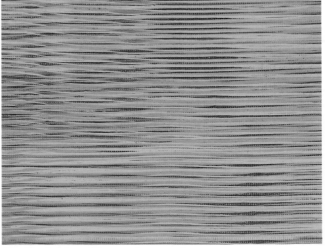

+ Dark blue and lilac

+ Dark yellow, lemon yellow and mid green

+ Dark blue, lilac and turquoise

Color Washing

Stencilling

+ Bright orange

+ Light green

+ Bright orange and dark yellow

+ Light green and turquoise

+ Bright orange, dark yellow and red

+ Light green, turquoise and dark blue

Frottage

Rag Rolling

⊕ Purple

⊕ Buff

⊕ Purple and lilac

⊕ Buff and terracotta

⊕ Purple, lilac and pink

⊕ Buff, terracotta and light gray

33

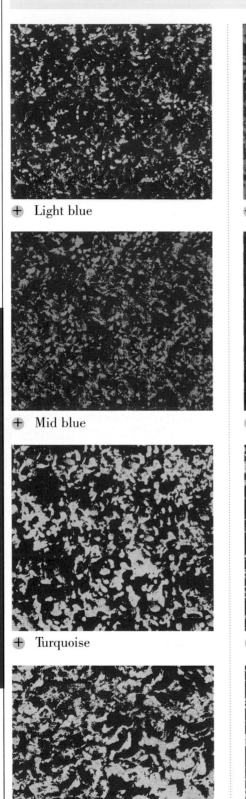

DARK BLUE

34

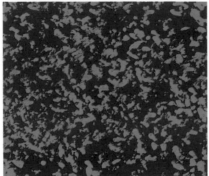

+ Light blue

+ Mid green

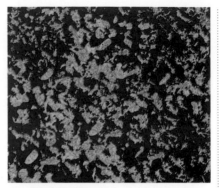

+ Dark yellow

+ Mid blue

+ Dark green

+ Bright orange

+ Turquoise

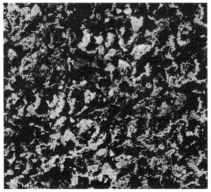

+ Cream

+ Red

+ Light green

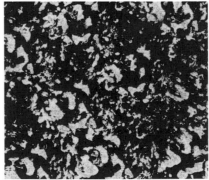

+ Lemon yellow

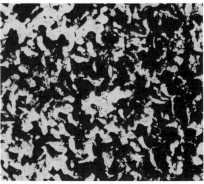

+ Pink

+ Peach

+ Purple

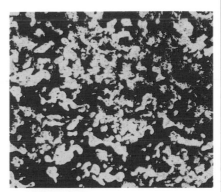

+ Light gray

+ Crimson red

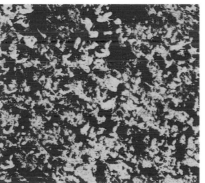

+ Buff

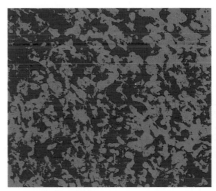

+ Dark gray

+ Burgundy

+ Terracotta

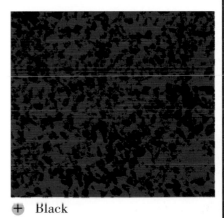

+ Black

+ Lilac

+ Brown

+ White

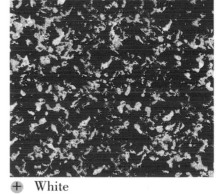

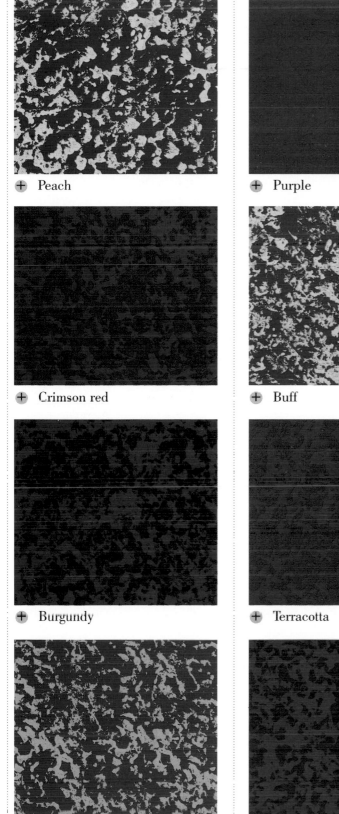

35

Dragging

Spattering

+ Dark gray

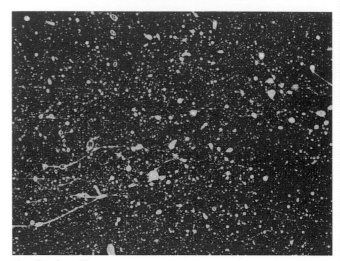

+ Dark yellow

+ Dark gray and mid blue

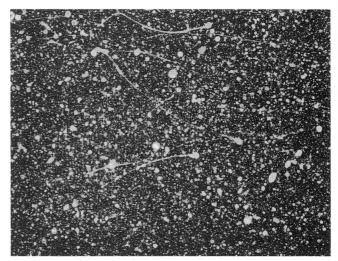

+ Dark yellow and light gray

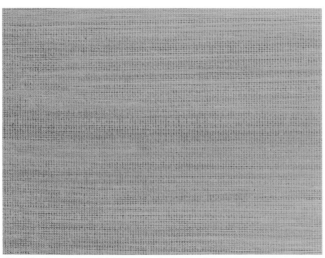

+ Dark gray, mid blue and turquoise

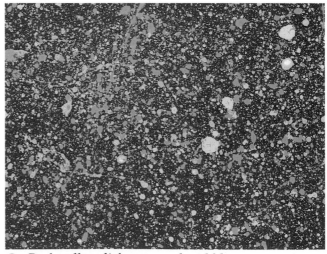

+ Dark yellow, light gray and mid blue

Stippling

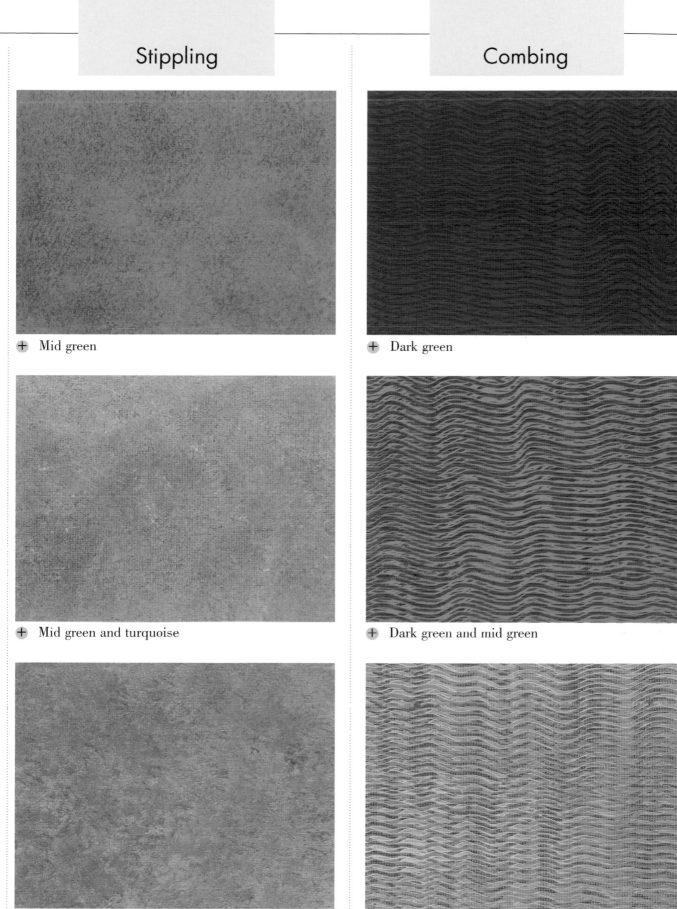

+ Mid green

+ Mid green and turquoise

+ Mid green, turquoise and dark green

Combing

+ Dark green

+ Dark green and mid green

+ Dark green, mid green and dark yellow

37

Color Washing

Stencilling

⊕ Purple

⊕ Dark yellow

⊕ Purple and lilac

⊕ Dark yellow and bright orange

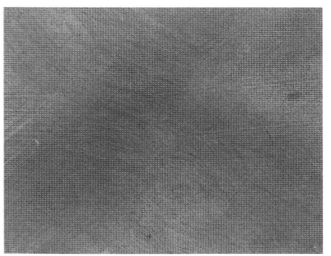

⊕ Purple, lilac and lemon yellow

⊕ Dark yellow, bright orange and red

Frottage

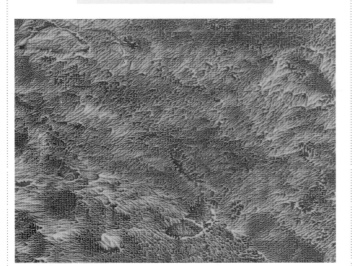

+ Light gray

+ Turquoise

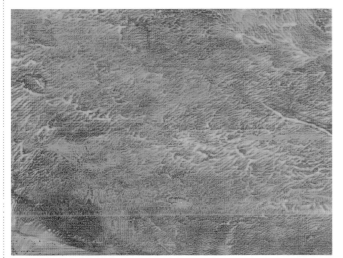

+ Light gray and lilac

+ Turquoise and light green

+ Light gray, lilac and purple

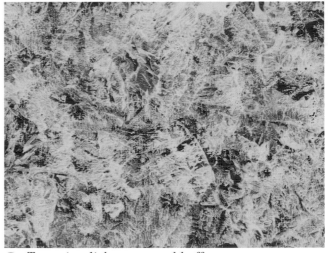

+ Turquoise, light green and buff

39

Sponging

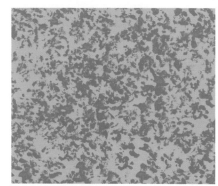

+ Light blue

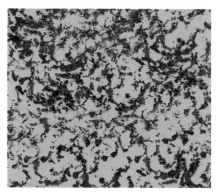

+ Mid green

+ Dark yellow

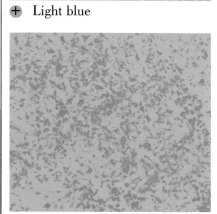

+ Mid blue

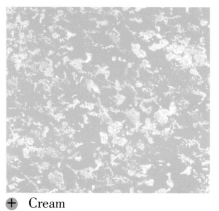

+ Dark green

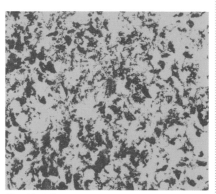

+ Bright orange

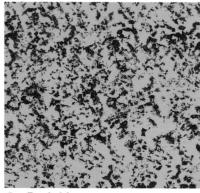

+ Dark blue

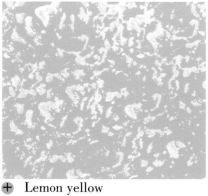

+ Cream

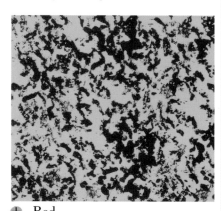

+ Red

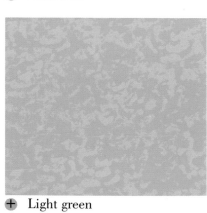

+ Light green

+ Lemon yellow

+ Pink

+ Peach

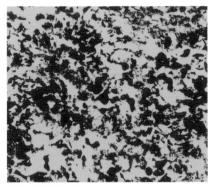
+ Purple

+ Light gray

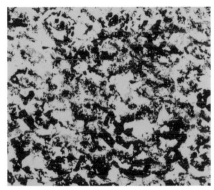
+ Crimson red

+ Buff

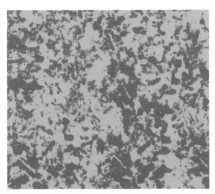
+ Dark gray

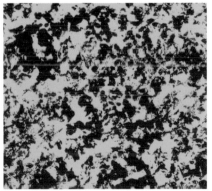
+ Burgundy

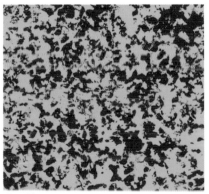
+ Terracotta

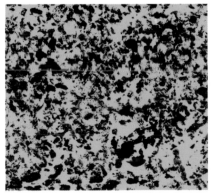
+ Black

+ Lilac

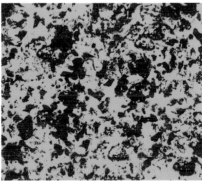
+ Brown

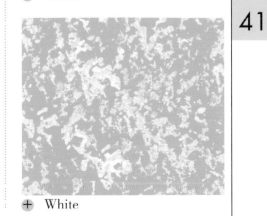
+ White

41

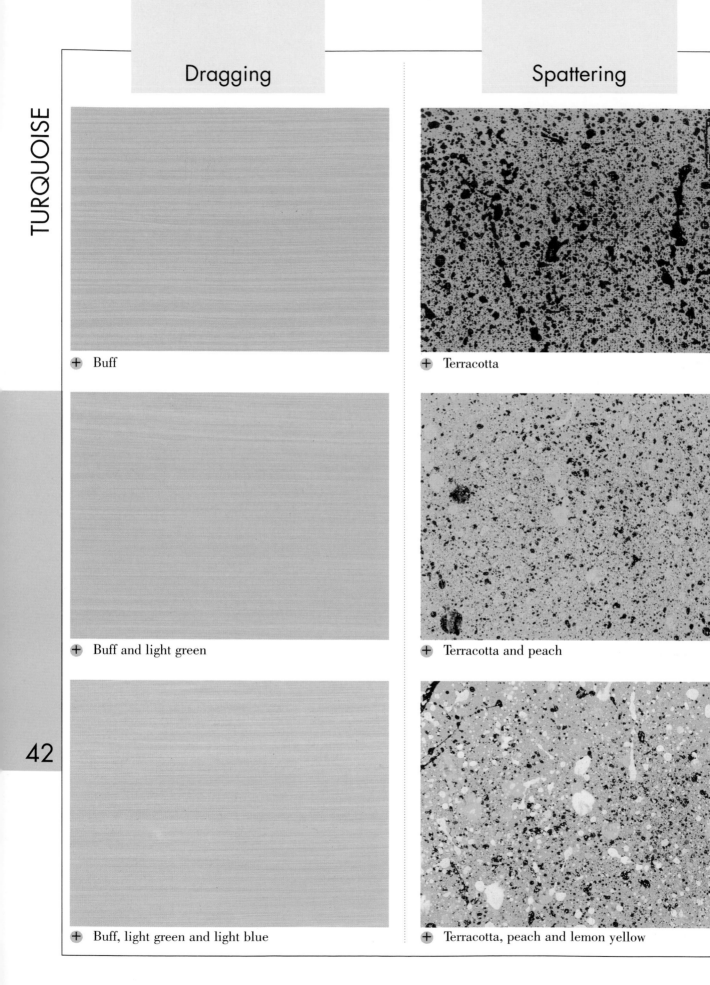

Dragging

Spattering

+ Buff

+ Terracotta

+ Buff and light green

+ Terracotta and peach

42

+ Buff, light green and light blue

+ Terracotta, peach and lemon yellow

Stippling

Combing

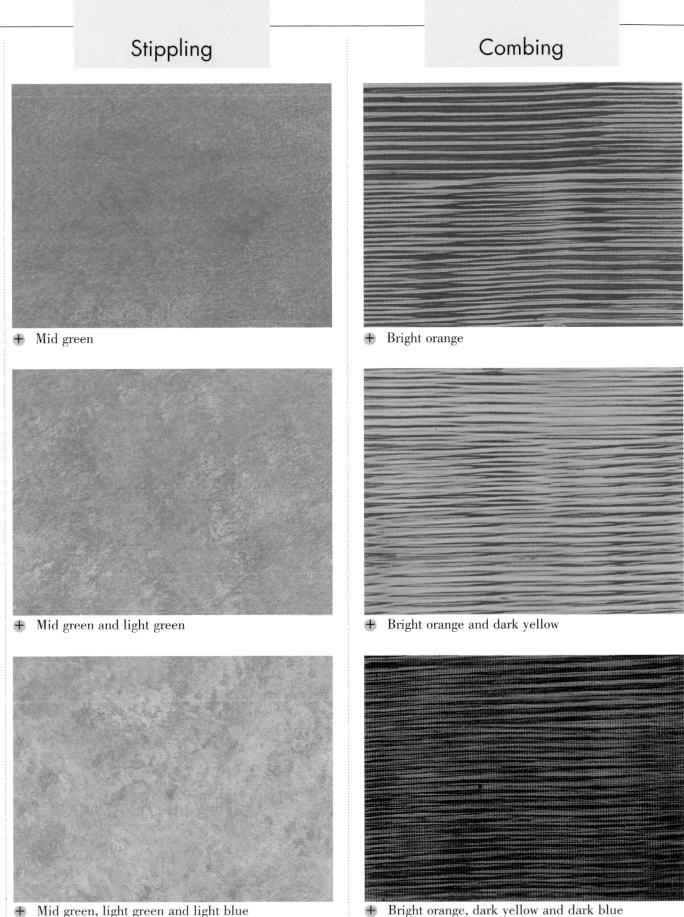

+ Mid green

+ Bright orange

+ Mid green and light green

+ Bright orange and dark yellow

+ Mid green, light green and light blue

+ Bright orange, dark yellow and dark blue

43

Color Washing

Stencilling

+ Lilac

+ Peach

+ Lilac and purple

+ Peach and mid blue

+ Lilac, purple and dark blue

+ Peach, mid blue and mid green

Frottage

Rag Rolling

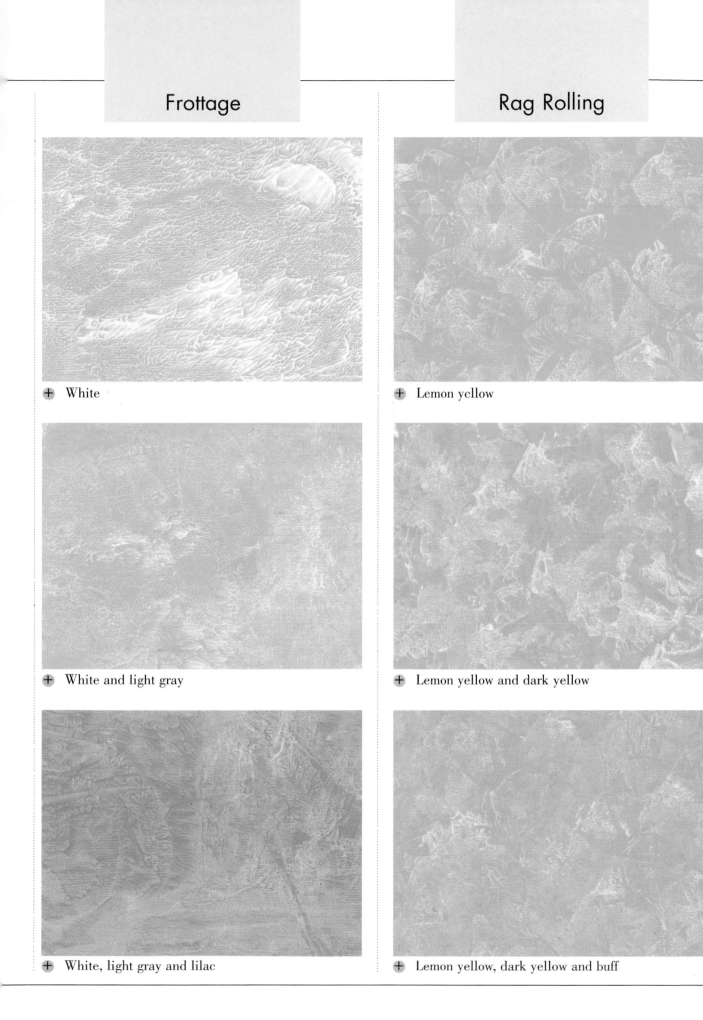

+ White

+ Lemon yellow

+ White and light gray

+ Lemon yellow and dark yellow

+ White, light gray and lilac

+ Lemon yellow, dark yellow and buff

45

Sponging

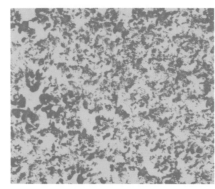

+ Light blue

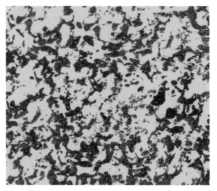

+ Mid green

+ Dark yellow

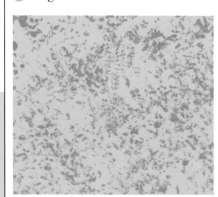

+ Mid blue

+ Dark green

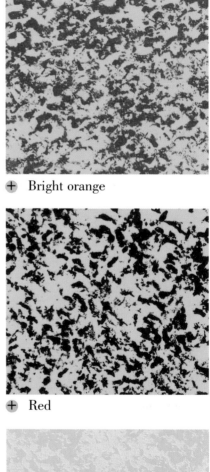

+ Bright orange

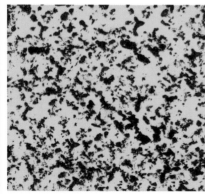

+ Dark blue

+ Cream

+ Red

+ Turquoise

+ Lemon yellow

+ Pink

⊕ Peach

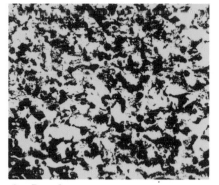

⊕ Purple

⊕ Light gray

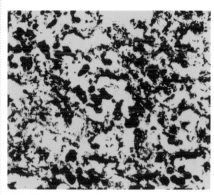

⊕ Crimson red

⊕ Buff

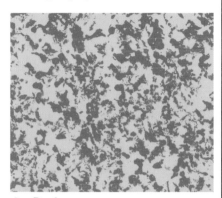

⊕ Dark gray

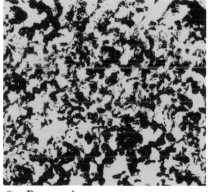

◐ Burgundy

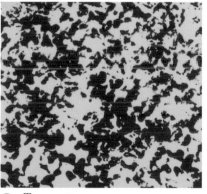

⊕ Terracotta

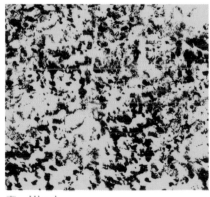

⊕ Black

⊕ Lilac

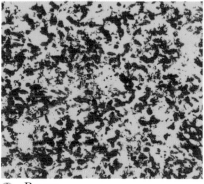

⊕ Brown

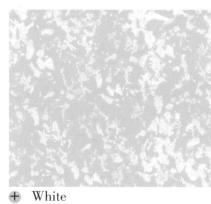

⊕ White

47

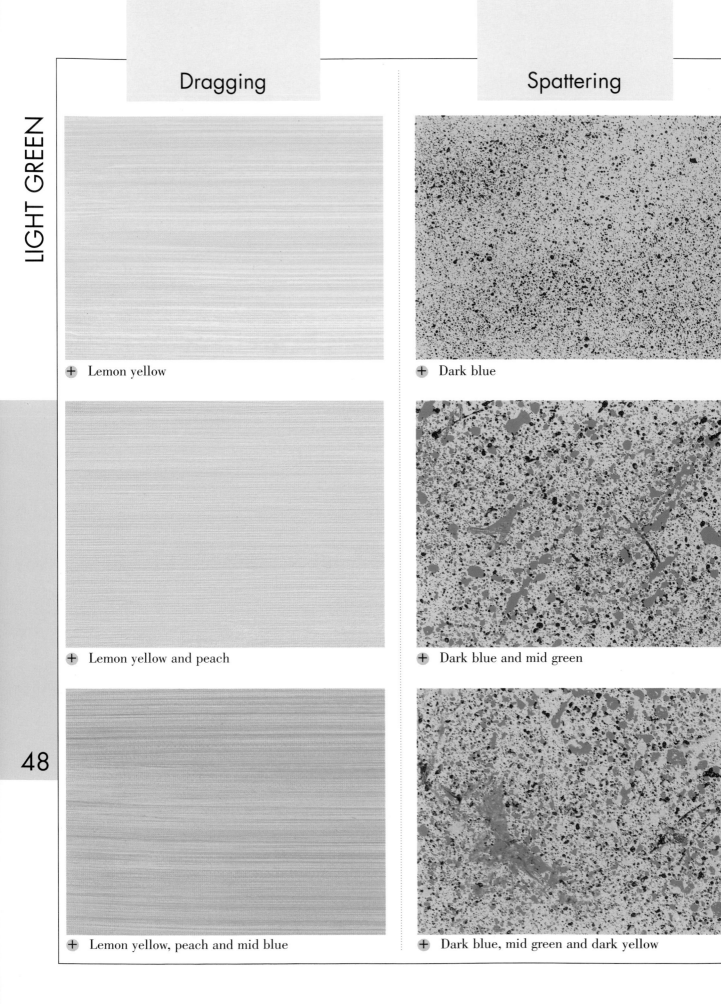

LIGHT GREEN

48

Dragging

+ Lemon yellow

+ Lemon yellow and peach

+ Lemon yellow, peach and mid blue

Spattering

+ Dark blue

+ Dark blue and mid green

+ Dark blue, mid green and dark yellow

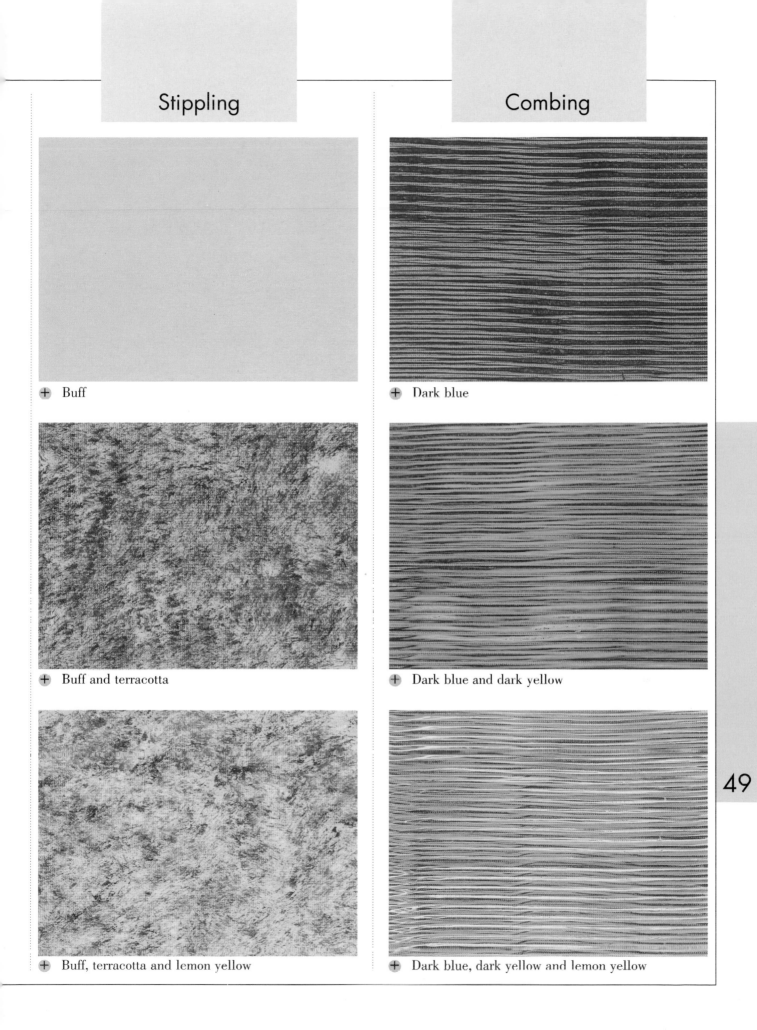

Stippling

+ Buff

+ Buff and terracotta

+ Buff, terracotta and lemon yellow

Combing

+ Dark blue

+ Dark blue and dark yellow

+ Dark blue, dark yellow and lemon yellow

49

Color Washing

Stencilling

+ Lilac

+ Mid green

+ Lilac and dark yellow

+ Mid green and peach

+ Lilac, dark yellow and cream

+ Mid green, peach and dark yellow

Frottage

Rag Rolling

+ Dark blue

+ Red

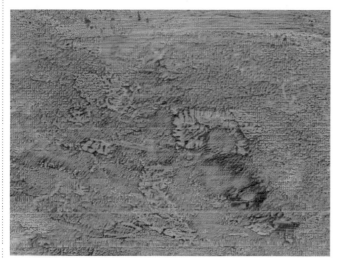

+ Dark blue and dark yellow

+ Red and turquoise

+ Dark blue, dark yellow and mid green

+ Red, turquoise and lemon yellow

51

MID GREEN

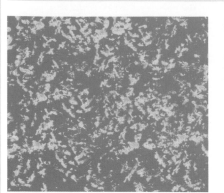

➕ Light blue

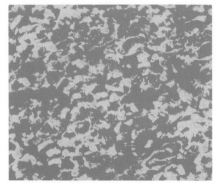

➕ Light green

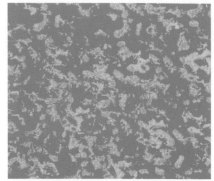

➕ Dark yellow

➕ Mid blue

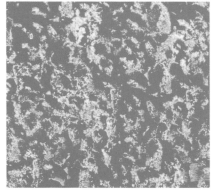

➕ Dark green

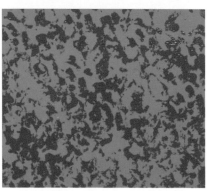

➕ Bright orange

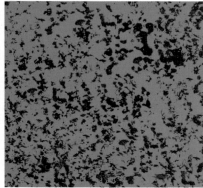

➕ Dark blue

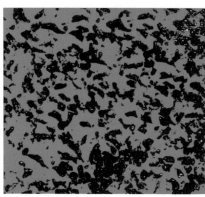

➕ Cream

➕ Red

52

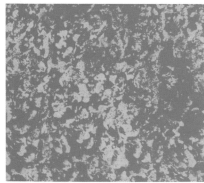

➕ Turquoise

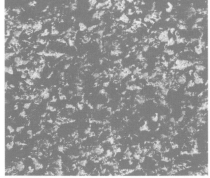

➕ Lemon yellow

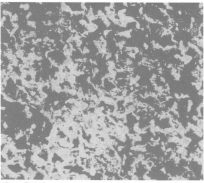

➕ Pink

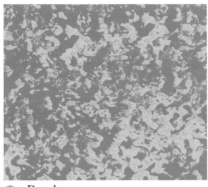

+ Peach

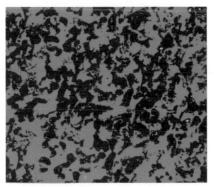

+ Purple

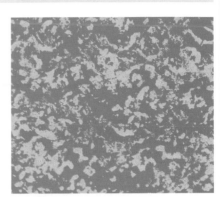

+ Light gray

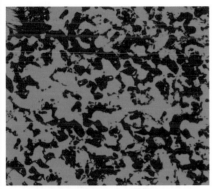

+ Crimson red

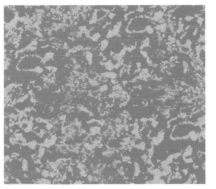

+ Buff

+ Dark gray

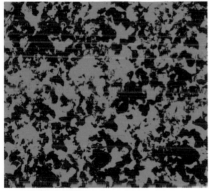

+ Burgundy

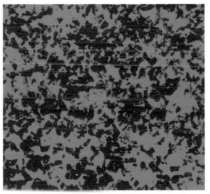

+ Terracotta

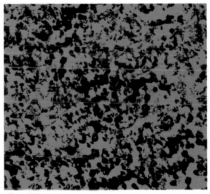

+ Black

+ Lilac

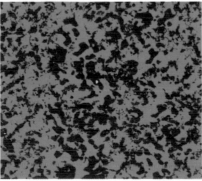

+ Brown

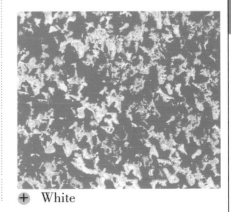

+ White

53

Dragging

Spattering

+ Purple

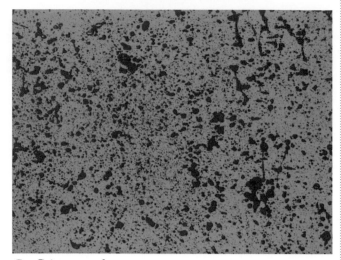

+ Crimson red

+ Purple and lilac

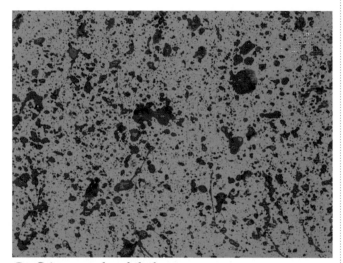

+ Crimson red and dark green

+ Purple, lilac and cream

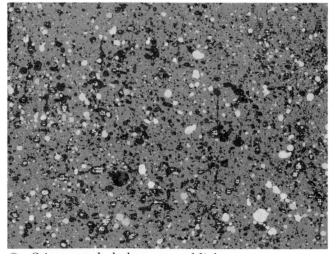

+ Crimson red, dark green and light green

Stippling

⊕ Dark yellow

⊕ Dark yellow and crimson red

⊕ Dark yellow, crimson red and bright orange

Combing

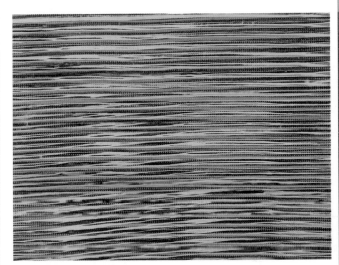

⊕ Black

⊕ Black and light gray

⊕ Black, light gray and red

Color Washing

Stencilling

+ Dark blue

+ Red

+ Dark blue and turquoise

+ Red and dark yellow

+ Dark blue, turquoise and mid blue

+ Red, dark yellow and peach

Frottage

Rag Rolling

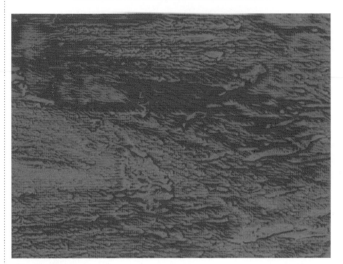

+ Bright orange

+ Dark blue

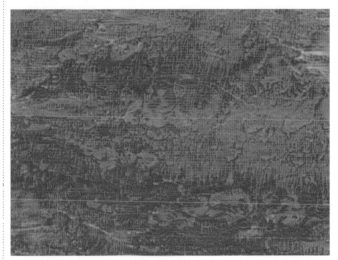

+ Bright orange and dark yellow

+ Dark blue and light green

+ Bright orange, dark yellow and dark green

+ Dark blue, light green and dark yellow

DARK GREEN

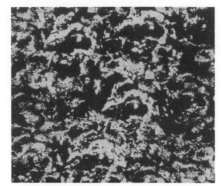

+ Light blue

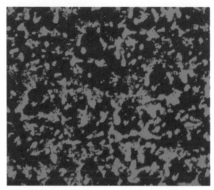

+ Light green

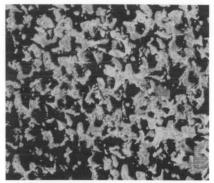

+ Dark yellow

+ Mid blue

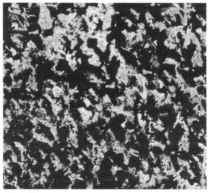

+ Mid green

+ Bright orange

Dark blue

+ Cream

+ Red

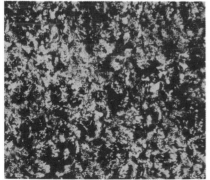

+ Turquoise

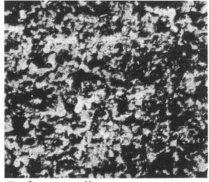

+ Lemon yellow

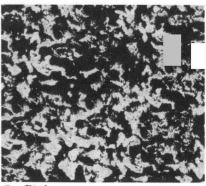

+ Pink

58

+ Peach

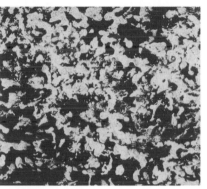

+ Purple

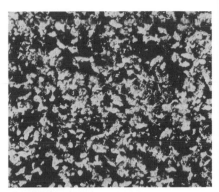

+ Light gray

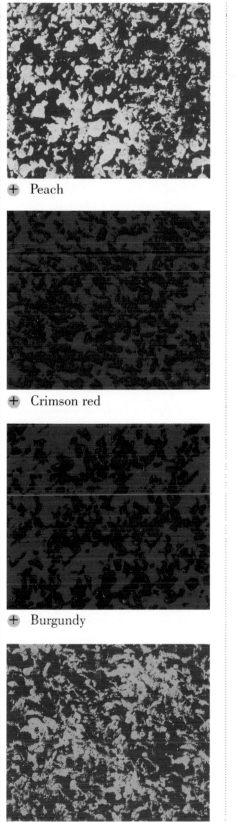

+ Crimson red

+ Buff

+ Dark gray

+ Burgundy

+ Terracotta

+ Black

+ Lilac

+ Brown

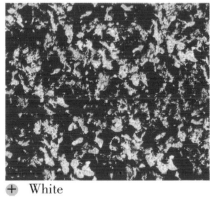

+ White

59

Dragging

Spattering

+ Mid green

+ Light gray

+ Mid green and dark yellow

+ Light gray and dark blue

+ Mid green, dark yellow and buff

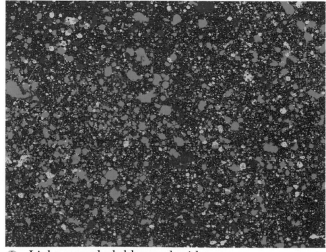

+ Light gray, dark blue and mid green

Stippling

Combing

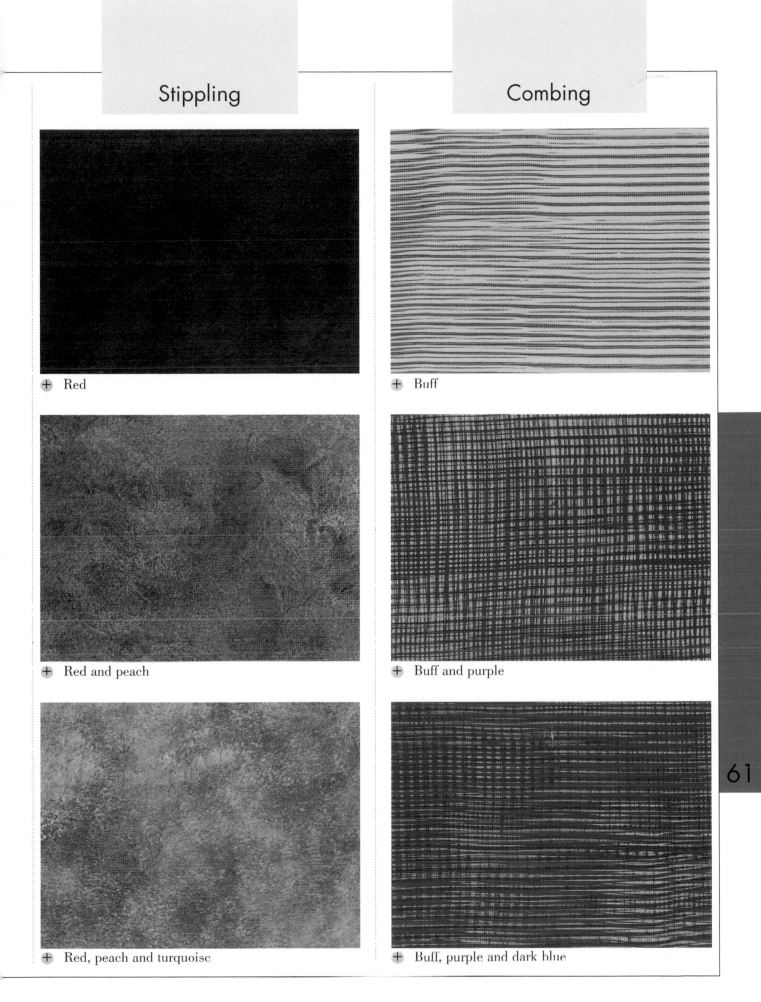

⊕ Red

⊕ Buff

⊕ Red and peach

⊕ Buff and purple

⊕ Red, peach and turquoise

⊕ Buff, purple and dark blue

61

Color Washing

Stencilling

+ Dark yellow

+ Purple

+ Dark yellow and crimson red

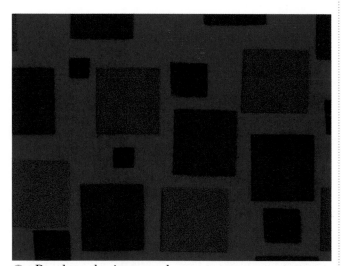

+ Purple and crimson red

+ Dark yellow, crimson red and purple

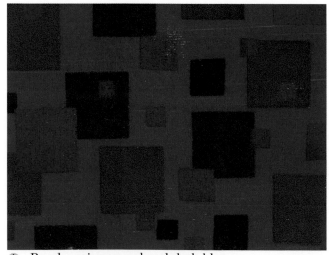

+ Purple, crimson red and dark blue

Frottage

Rag Rolling

+ Dark blue

+ Terracotta

+ Dark blue and turquoise

+ Terracotta and buff

+ Dark blue, turquoise and light gray

+ Terracotta, buff and burgundy

Sponging

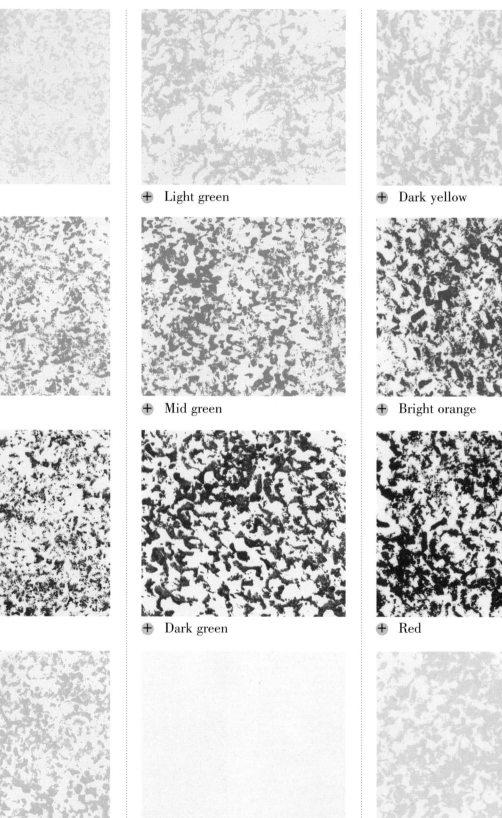

+ Light blue

+ Light green

+ Dark yellow

+ Mid blue

+ Mid green

+ Bright orange

+ Dark blue

+ Dark green

+ Red

+ Turquoise

+ Lemon yellow

+ Pink

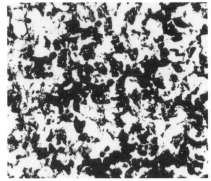

➕ Peach

➕ Purple

➕ Light gray

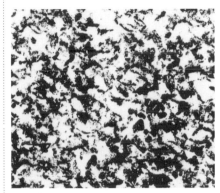

➕ Crimson red

➕ Buff

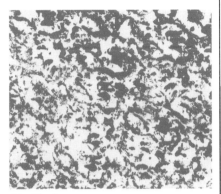

➕ Dark gray

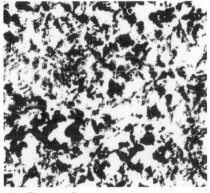

➕ Burgundy

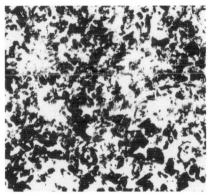

➕ Terracotta

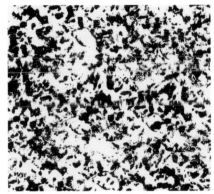

➕ Black

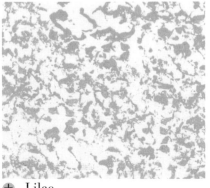

➕ Lilac

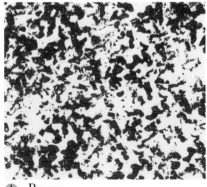

➕ Brown

➕ White

65

Dragging

Spattering

+ Dark yellow

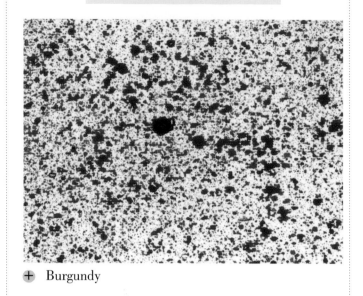

+ Burgundy

+ Dark yellow and mid blue

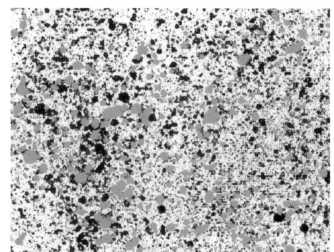

+ Burgundy and lilac

+ Dark yellow, mid blue and dark blue

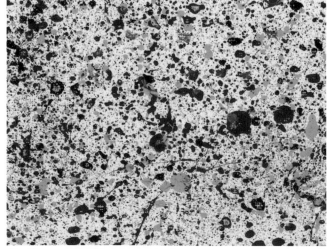

+ Burgundy, lilac and purple

66

Stippling

Combing

+ Mid green

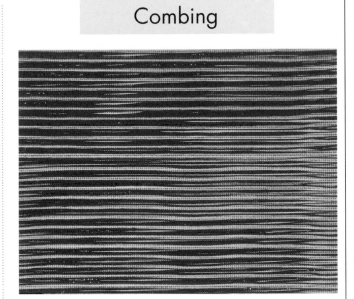

+ Brown

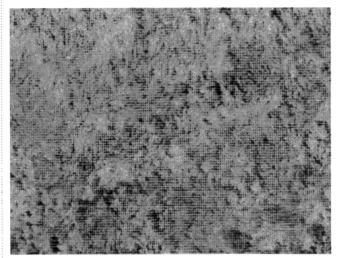

+ Mid green and black

+ Brown and buff

+ Mid green, black and buff

+ Brown, buff and lemon yellow

67

Color Washing

Stencilling

+ Light green

+ Pink

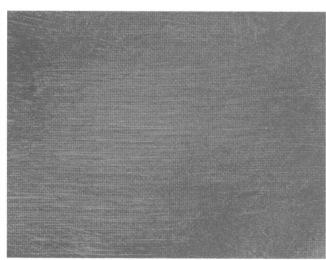

+ Light green and mid blue

+ Pink and lilac

+ Light green, mid blue and peach

+ Pink, lilac and turquoise

Frottage

⊕ Dark blue

⊕ Dark blue and mid green

⊕ Dark blue, mid green and dark yellow

Rag Rolling

⊕ Light blue

⊕ Light blue and peach

⊕ Light blue and peach and light gray

LEMON YELLOW

+ Light blue

+ Light green

+ Dark yellow

+ Mid blue

+ Mid green

+ Bright orange

+ Dark blue

+ Dark green

+ Red

70

+ Turquoise

+ Cream

+ Pink

+ Peach

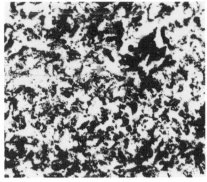

+ Purple

+ Light gray

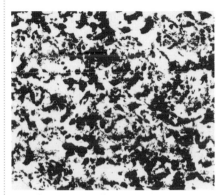

+ Crimson red

+ Buff

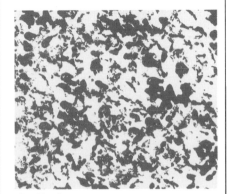

+ Dark gray

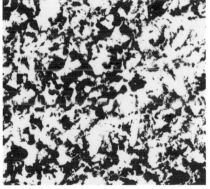

+ Burgundy

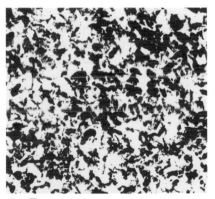

+ Terracotta

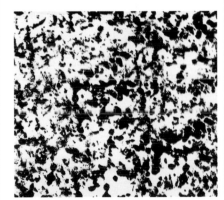

+ Black

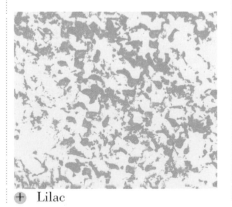

+ Lilac

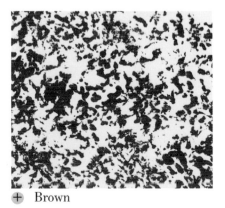

+ Brown

+ White

71

Dragging

Spattering

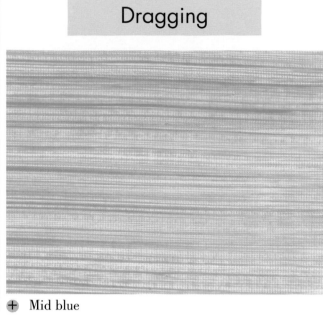

⊕ Mid blue

⊕ Mid blue and light blue

⊕ Mid blue, light blue and white

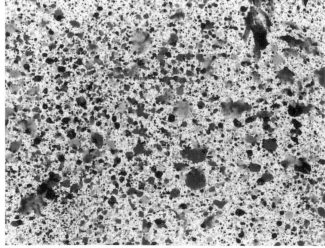

⊕ Red

⊕ Red and bright orange

⊕ Red, bright orange and dark yellow

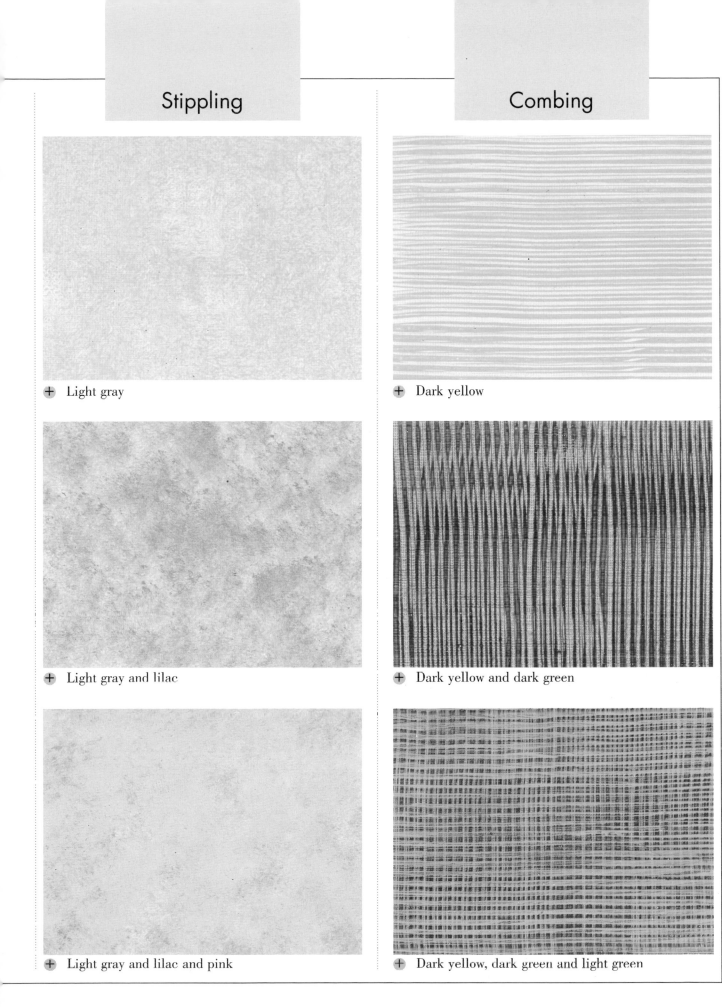

Stippling

+ Light gray

+ Light gray and lilac

+ Light gray and lilac and pink

Combing

+ Dark yellow

+ Dark yellow and dark green

+ Dark yellow, dark green and light green

73

LEMON YELLOW

Color Washing

Stencilling

+ Lilac

+ Dark yellow

+ Lilac and mid green

+ Dark yellow and dark green

74

+ Lilac and mid green and turquoise

+ Dark yellow, dark green and mid green

Frottage

Rag Rolling

+ Light blue

+ Light gray

+ Light blue and pink

+ Light gray and dark yellow

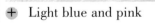

+ Light blue, pink and lemon yellow

+ Light gray, dark yellow and turquoise

Sponging

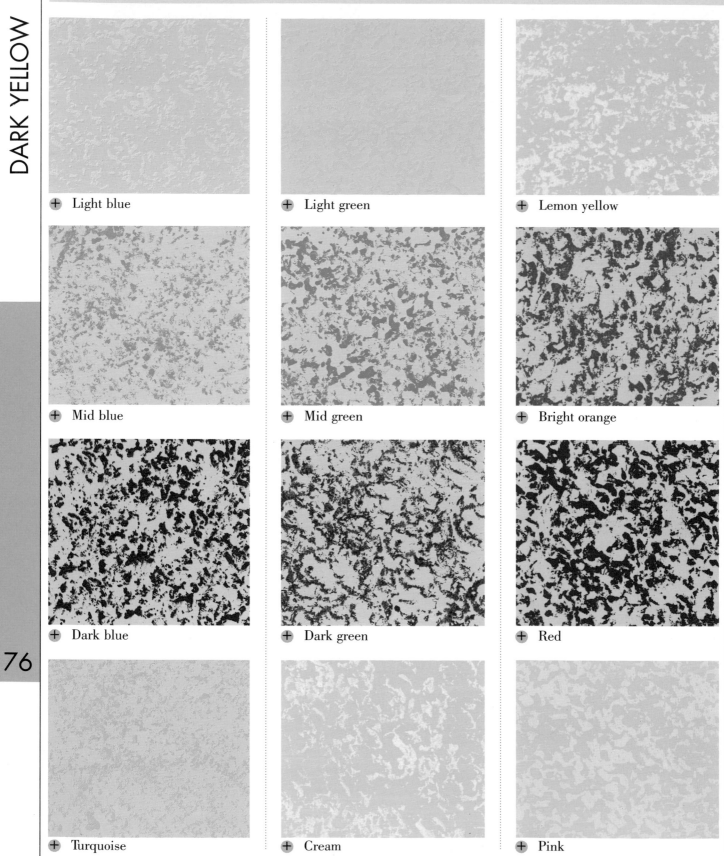

+ Light blue

+ Light green

+ Lemon yellow

+ Mid blue

+ Mid green

+ Bright orange

+ Dark blue

+ Dark green

+ Red

+ Turquoise

+ Cream

+ Pink

⊕ Peach

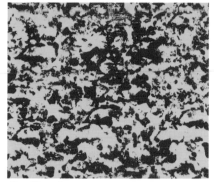

⊕ Purple

⊕ Light gray

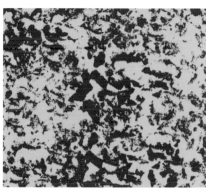

⊕ Crimson red

⊕ Buff

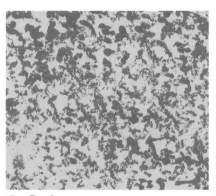

⊕ Dark gray

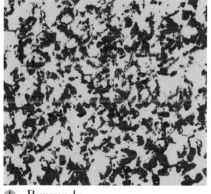

⊕ Burgundy

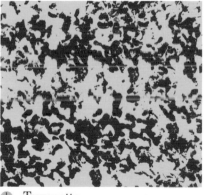

⊕ Terracotta

⊕ Black

⊕ Lilac

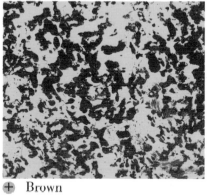

⊕ Brown

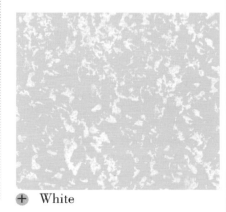

⊕ White

Dragging

Spattering

+ Red

+ Turquoise

+ Red and bright orange

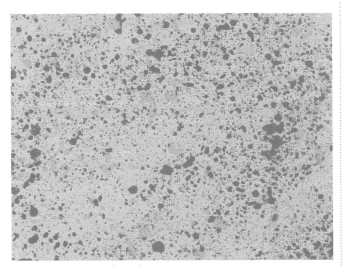

+ Turquoise and mid green

+ Red, bright orange and lemon yellow

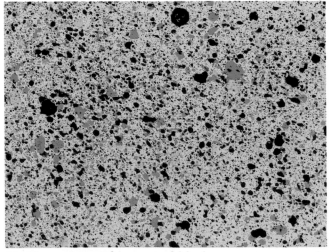

+ Turquoise, mid green and black

Stippling

+ Cream

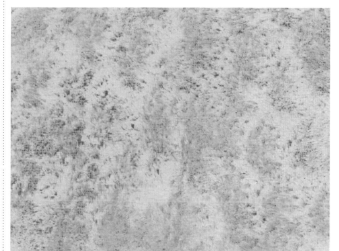

+ Cream and bright orange

+ Cream, bright orange and dark blue

Combing

+ Light blue

+ Light blue and lilac

+ Light blue, lilac and mid green

79

Color Washing

Stencilling

+ Light green

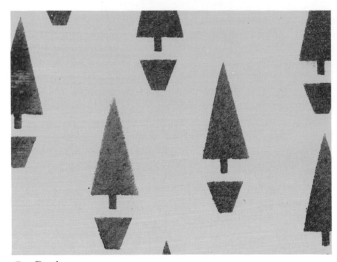

+ Dark green

+ Light green and peach

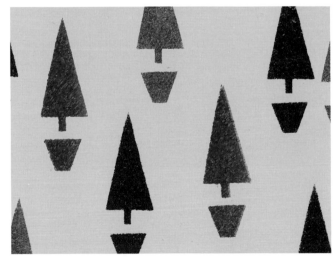

+ Dark green and dark blue

+ Light green, peach and lilac

+ Dark green, dark blue and crimson red

Frottage

Rag Rolling

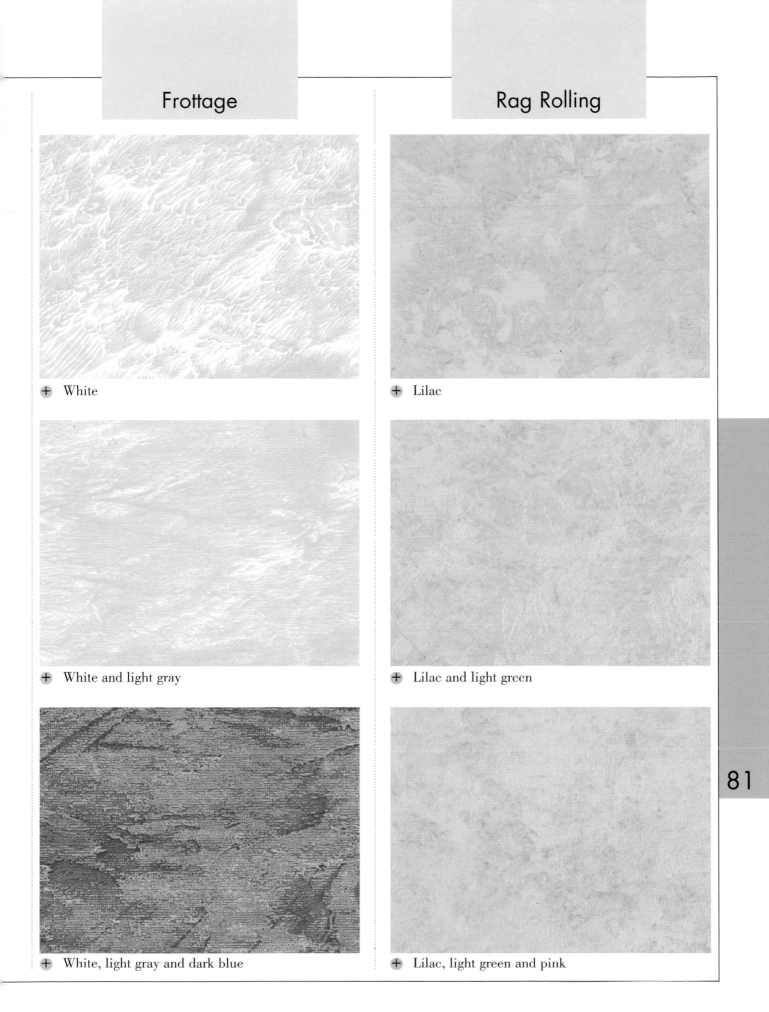

+ White

+ Lilac

+ White and light gray

+ Lilac and light green

+ White, light gray and dark blue

+ Lilac, light green and pink

81

Sponging

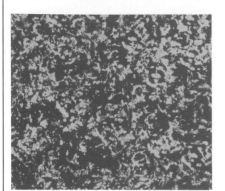

⊕ Light blue

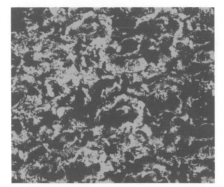

⊕ Light green

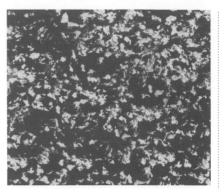

⊕ Lemon yellow

⊕ Mid blue

⊕ Mid green

⊕ Dark yellow

⊕ Dark blue

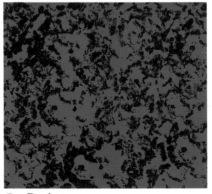

⊕ Dark green

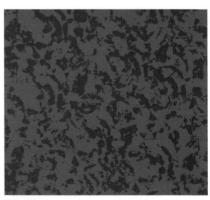

⊕ Red

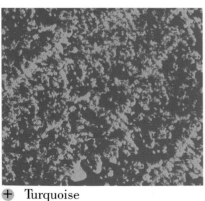

⊕ Turquoise

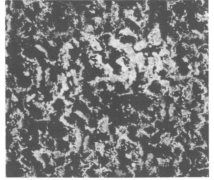

⊕ Cream

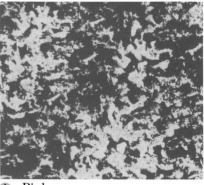

⊕ Pink

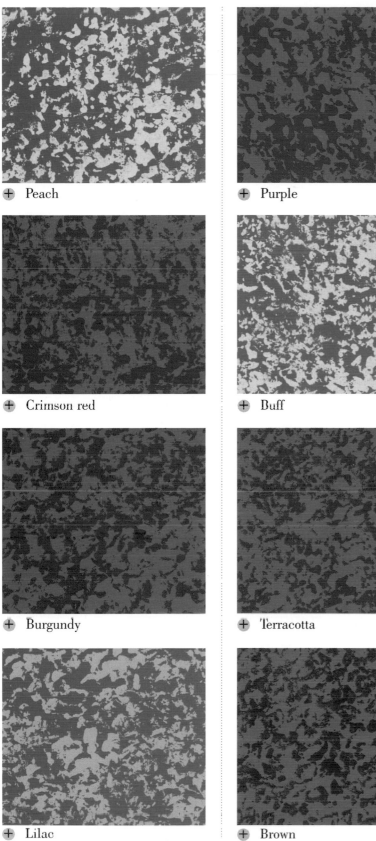

⊕ Peach

⊕ Purple

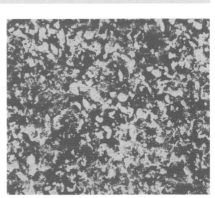

⊕ Light gray

⊕ Crimson red

⊕ Buff

⊕ Dark gray

⊕ Burgundy

⊕ Terracotta

⊕ Black

⊕ Lilac

⊕ Brown

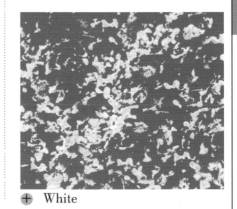

⊕ White

Dragging

Spattering

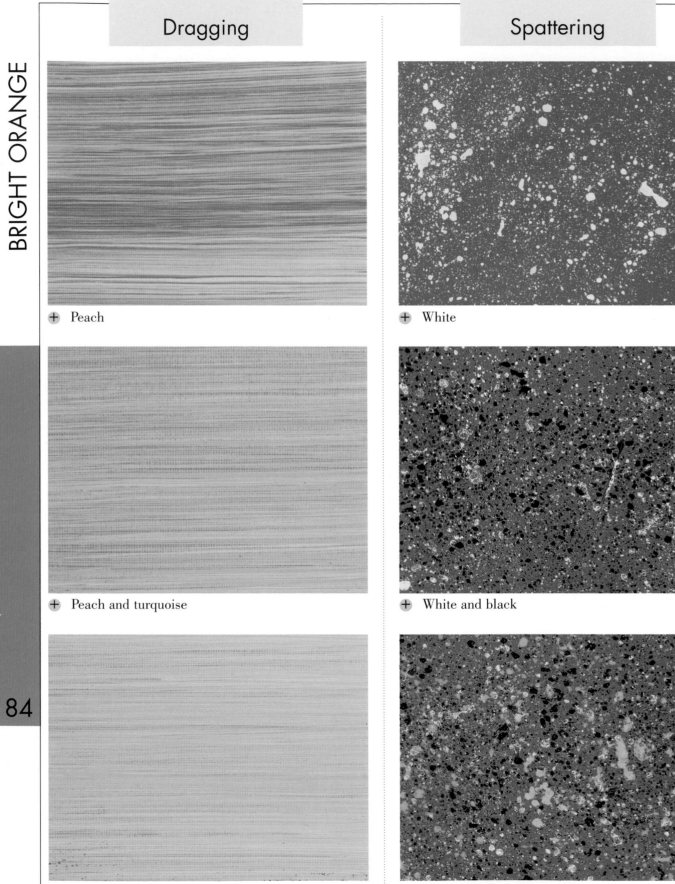

+ Peach

+ White

+ Peach and turquoise

+ White and black

+ Peach, turquoise and light grey

+ White, black and dark yellow

Stippling

Combing

+ Dark yellow

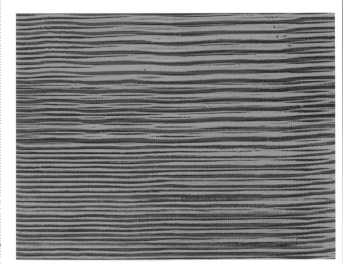

+ Purple

+ Dark yellow and mid green

+ Purple and lilac

+ Dark yellow, mid green and light blue

+ Purple, lilac and pink

Color Washing

Stencilling

+ Burgundy

+ Mid green

+ Burgundy and dark yellow

+ Mid green and dark green

+ Burgundy, dark yellow and cream

+ Mid green, dark green and dark yellow

Frottage

Rag Rolling

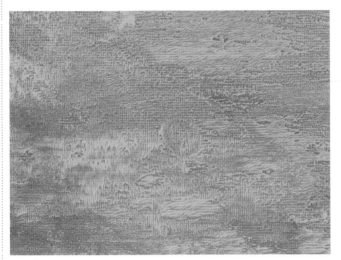

+ Light green

+ Red

+ Light green and buff

+ Red and dark blue

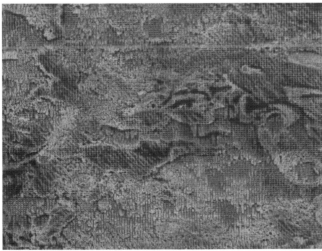

+ Light green, buff and burgundy

+ Red, dark blue and buff

Sponging

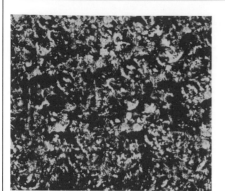

➕ Light blue

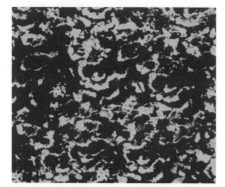

➕ Light green

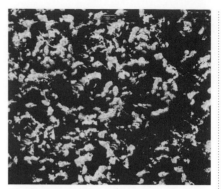

➕ Lemon yellow

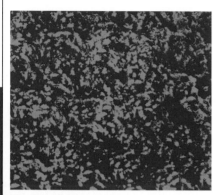

➕ Mid blue

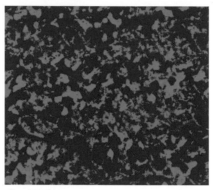

➕ Mid green

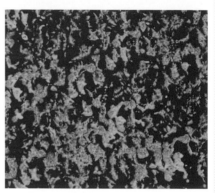

➕ Dark yellow

➕ Dark blue

➕ Dark green

➕ Bright orange

➕ Turquoise

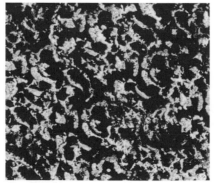

➕ Cream

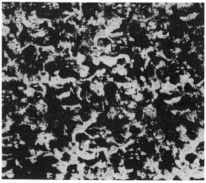

➕ Pink

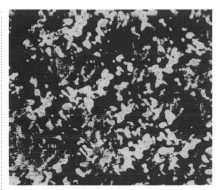

+ Peach

+ Purple

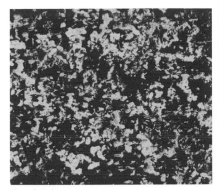

+ Light gray

+ Crimson red

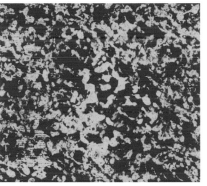

+ Buff

+ Dark gray

+ Burgundy

+ Terracotta

+ Black

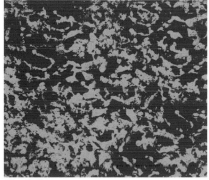

+ Lilac

+ Brown

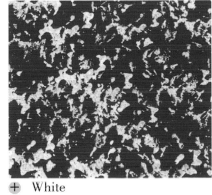

+ White

89

Dragging

Spattering

⊕ Purple

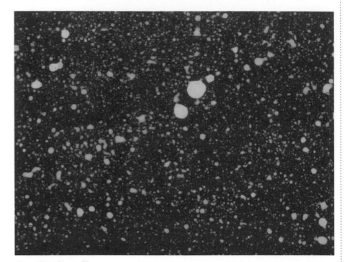

⊕ Dark yellow

⊕ Purple and lilac

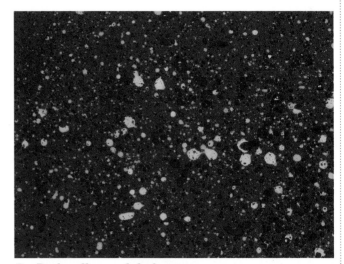

⊕ Dark yellow and dark green

⊕ Purple, lilac and peach

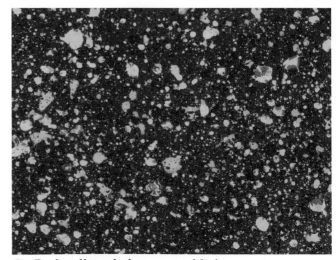

⊕ Dark yellow, dark green and light gray

Stippling

Combing

⊕ Peach

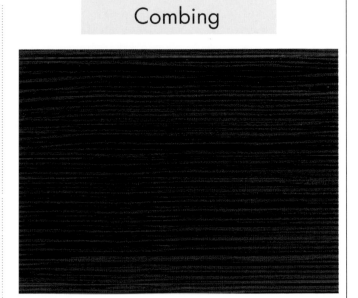

⊕ Black

⊕ Peach and mid green

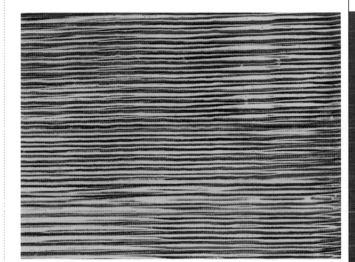

⊕ Black and peach

⊕ Peach, mid green and light green

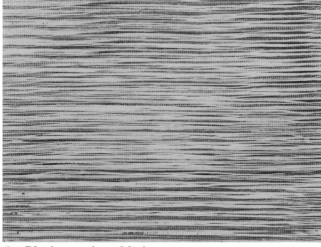

⊕ Black, peach and light gray

Color Washing

Stencilling

+ Burgundy

+ Dark blue

+ Burgundy and bright orange

+ Dark blue and dark yellow

+ Burgundy, bright orange and dark blue

+ Dark blue, dark yellow and white

Frottage

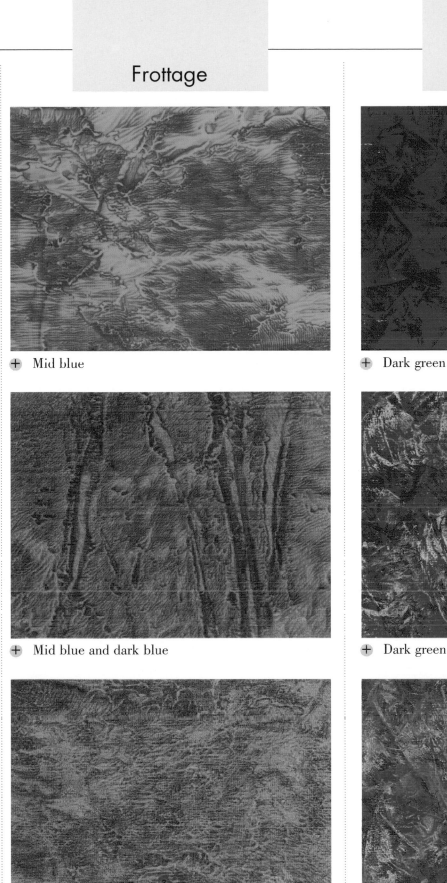

+ Mid blue

+ Mid blue and dark blue

| Mid blue, dark blue and dark yellow

Rag Rolling

+ Dark green

+ Dark green and light green

+ Dark green, light green and bright orange

93

Sponging

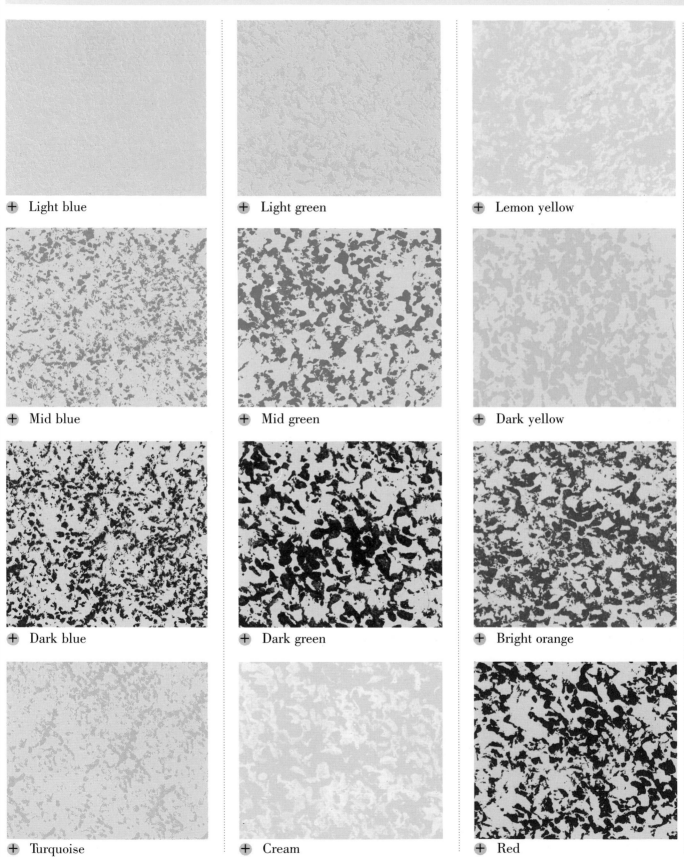

+ Light blue

+ Light green

+ Lemon yellow

+ Mid blue

+ Mid green

+ Dark yellow

+ Dark blue

+ Dark green

+ Bright orange

+ Turquoise

+ Cream

+ Red

⊕ Peach

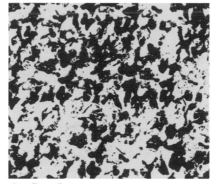

⊕ Purple

Light gray

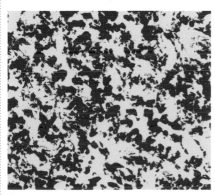

⊕ Crimson red

⊕ Buff

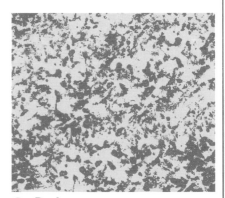

⊕ Dark gray

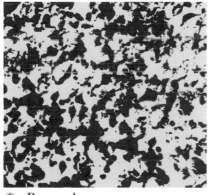

⊕ Burgundy

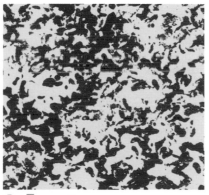

⊕ Terracotta

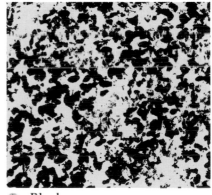

⊕ Black

95

⊕ Lilac

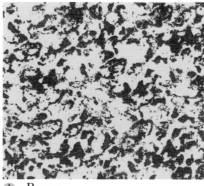

⊕ Brown

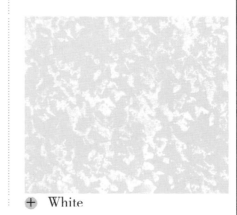

⊕ White

Dragging

Spattering

+ Light gray

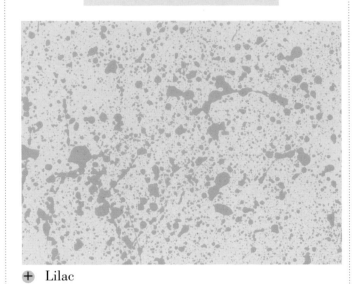

+ Lilac

+ Light gray and lilac

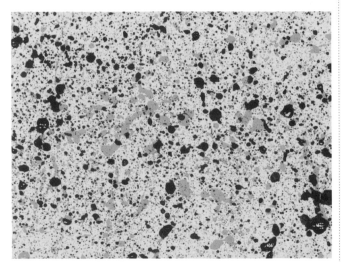

+ Lilac and purple

+ Light gray, lilac and light blue

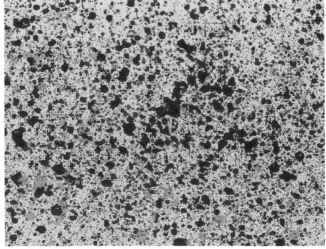

+ Lilac, purple and dark blue

Stippling

+ Light gray

+ Light gray and lemon yellow

+ Light gray, lemon yellow and light green

Combing

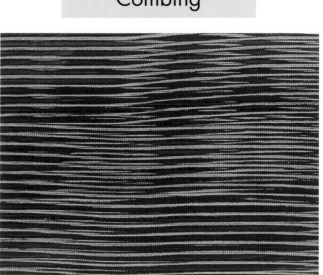

+ Dark blue

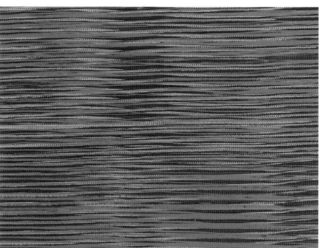

+ Dark blue and mid blue

+ Dark blue, mid blue and cream

Color Washing

Stencilling

+ Burgundy

+ Turquoise

+ Burgundy and purple

+ Turquoise and light blue

+ Burgundy, purple and dark blue

+ Turquoise, light blue and lilac

Frottage

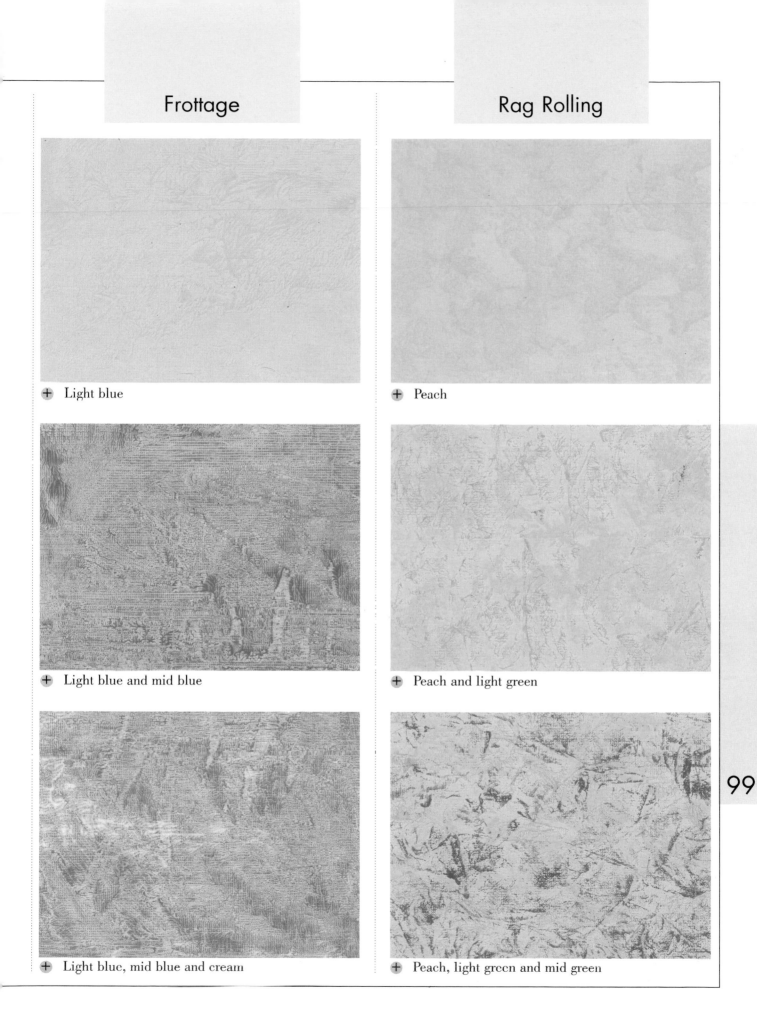

+ Light blue

+ Light blue and mid blue

+ Light blue, mid blue and cream

Rag Rolling

+ Peach

+ Peach and light green

+ Peach, light green and mid green

Sponging

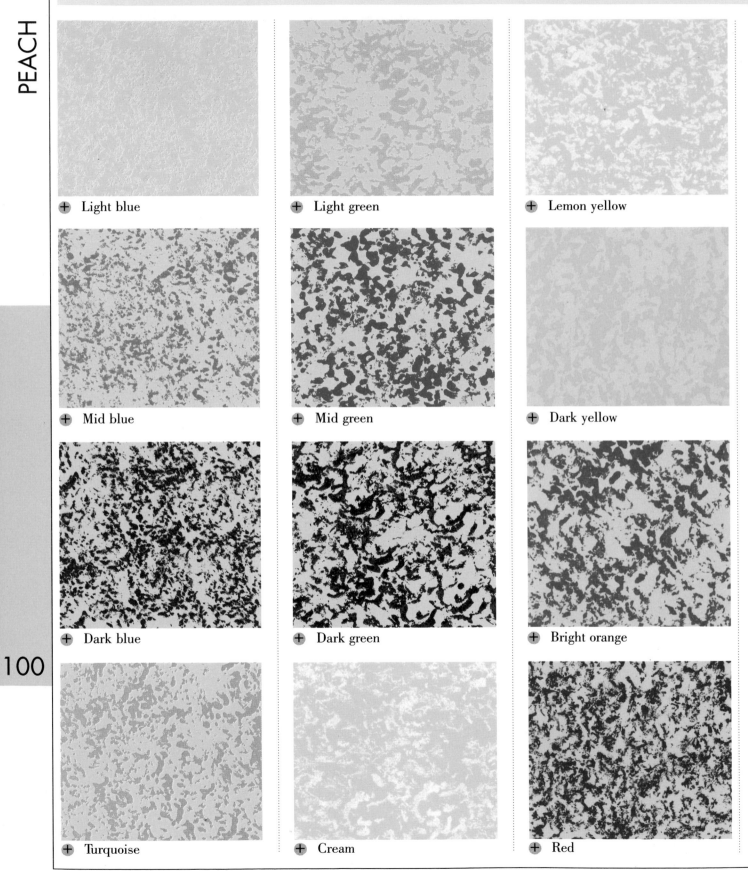

⊕ Light blue ⊕ Light green ⊕ Lemon yellow

⊕ Mid blue ⊕ Mid green ⊕ Dark yellow

⊕ Dark blue ⊕ Dark green ⊕ Bright orange

⊕ Turquoise ⊕ Cream ⊕ Red

 ⊕ Pink

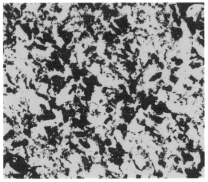 ⊕ Purple

 ⊕ Light gray

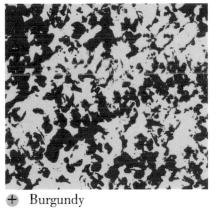 ⊕ Crimson red

 ⊕ Buff

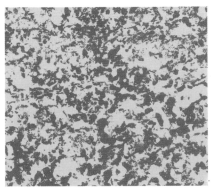 ⊕ Dark gray

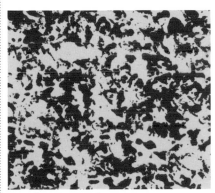 ⊕ Burgundy

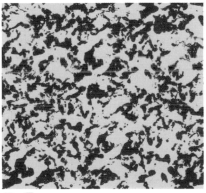 ⊕ Terracotta

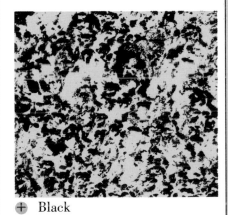 ⊕ Black

 ⊕ Lilac

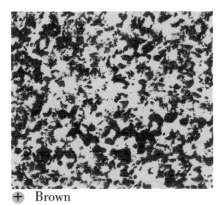 ⊕ Brown

⊕ White

101

Dragging

Spattering

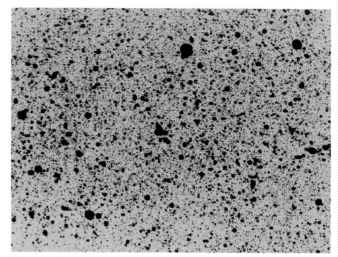

+ Light green

+ Black

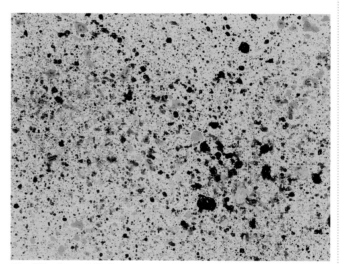

+ Light green and mid blue

+ Black and light gray

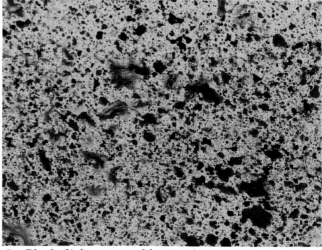

+ Light green, mid blue and dark yellow

+ Black, light gray and burgundy

Stippling

Combing

+ Mid blue

+ Bright orange

+ Mid blue and mid green

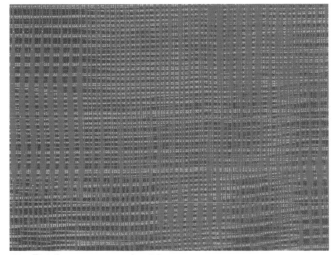

+ Bright orange and mid green

+ Mid blue, mid green and buff

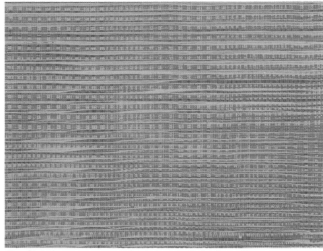

+ Bright orange, mid green and dark yellow

Color Washing

Stencilling

+ Light gray

+ Lilac

+ Light gray and red

+ Lilac and mid blue

+ Light gray, red and turquoise

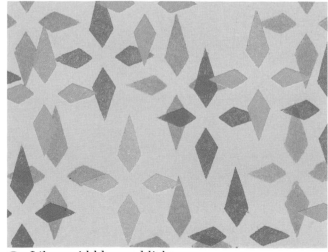

+ Lilac, mid blue and light green

Frottage

Rag Rolling

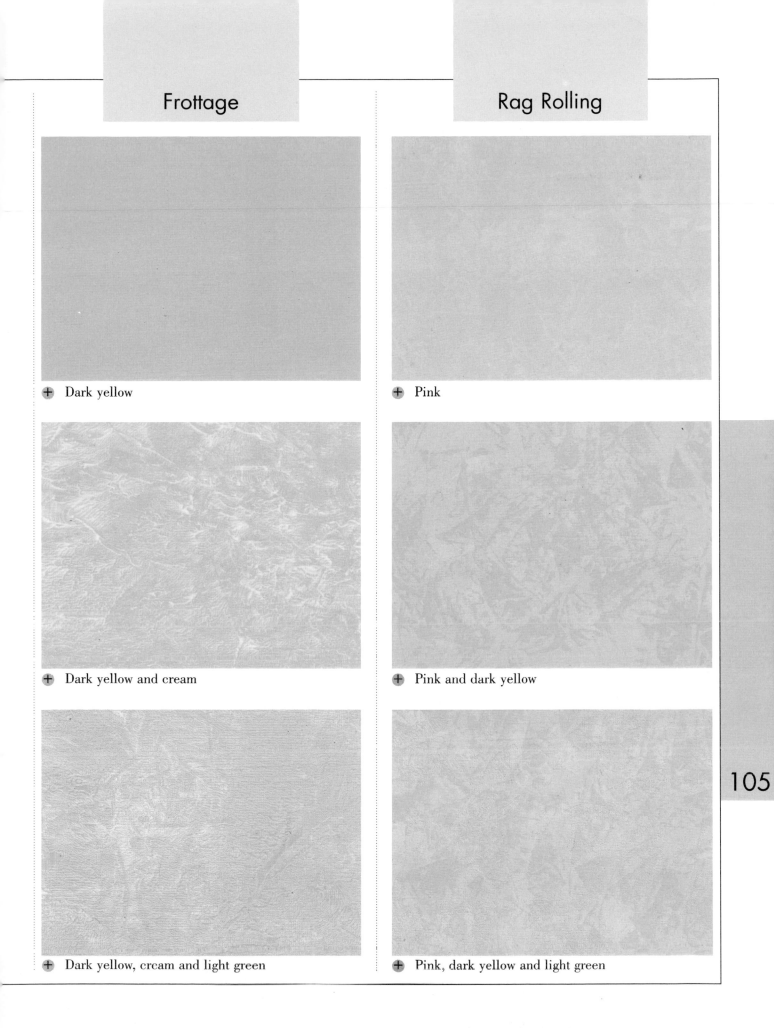

✛ Dark yellow

✛ Pink

✛ Dark yellow and cream

✛ Pink and dark yellow

✛ Dark yellow, cream and light green

✛ Pink, dark yellow and light green

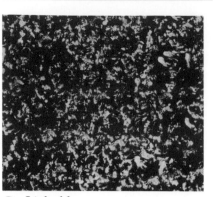

⊕ Light blue

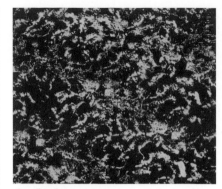

⊕ Light green

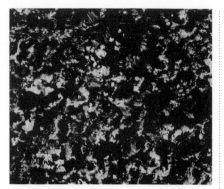

⊕ Lemon yellow

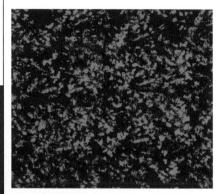

⊕ Mid blue

⊕ Mid green

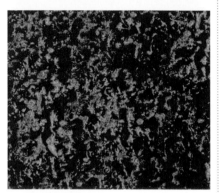

⊕ Dark yellow

⊕ Dark blue

⊕ Dark green

⊕ Bright orange

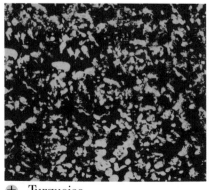

⊕ Turquoise

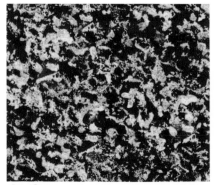

⊕ Cream

⊕ Red

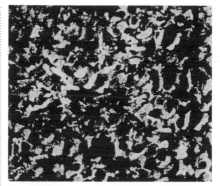

+ Pink

+ Purple

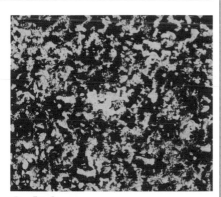

+ Light gray

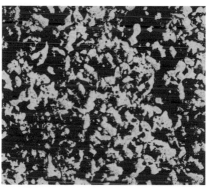

+ Peach

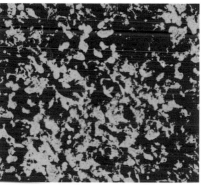

+ Buff

+ Dark gray

+ Burgundy

+ Terracotta

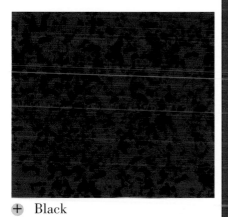

+ Black

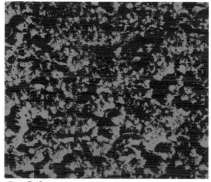

+ Lilac

+ Brown

+ White

Dragging

Spattering

⊕ Mid green

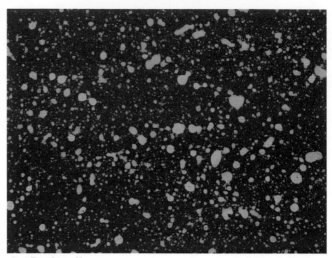

⊕ Dark yellow

⊕ Mid green and dark green

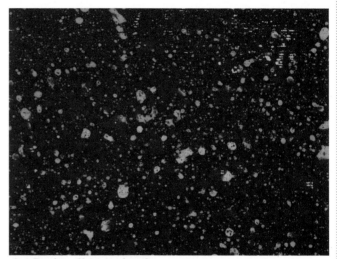

⊕ Dark yellow and red

⊕ Mid green and dark green and light green

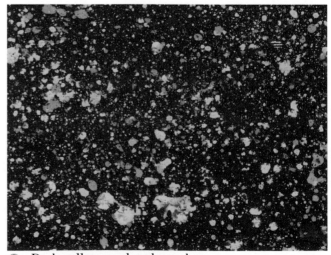

⊕ Dark yellow , red and peach

Stippling

⊕ Dark blue

⊕ Dark blue and mid blue

⊕ Dark blue, mid blue and purple

Combing

⊕ Burgundy

⊕ Burgundy and dark green

⊕ Burgundy, dark green and purple

Color Washing

Stencilling

+ Buff

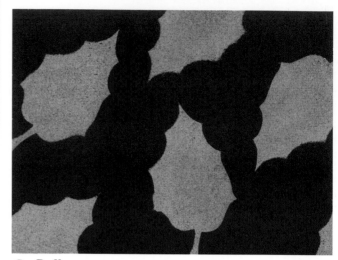

+ Buff

+ Buff and mid green

+ Buff and purple

+ Buff, mid green and turquoise

+ Buff, purple and mid green

Frottage

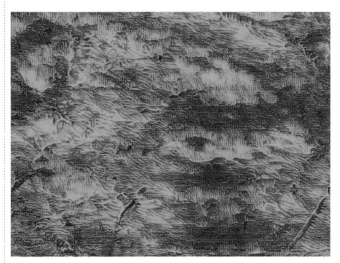

⊕ Turquoise

⊕ Turquoise and dark blue

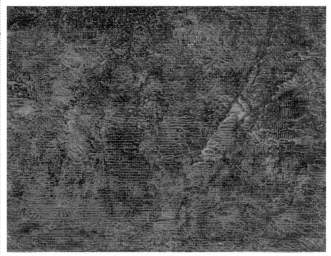

⊕ Turquoise, dark blue and dark yellow

Rag Rolling

⊕ Dark gray

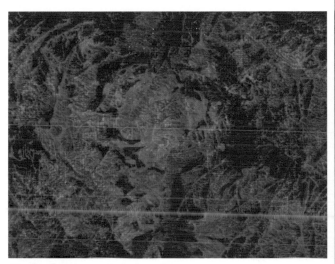

⊕ Dark gray and dark yellow

⊕ Dark gray, dark yellow and dark blue

Sponging

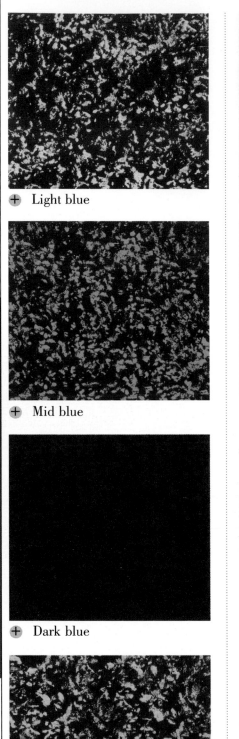

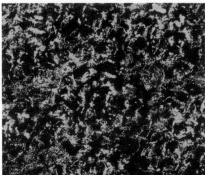

+ Light blue

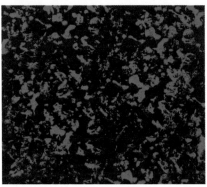

+ Light green

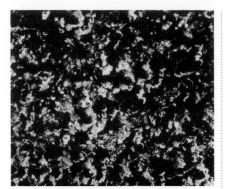

+ Lemon yellow

+ Mid blue

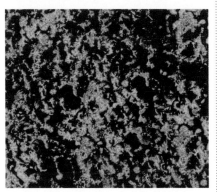

+ Mid green

+ Dark yellow

+ Dark blue

+ Dark green

+ Bright orange

+ Turquoise

+ Cream

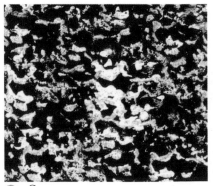

+ Red

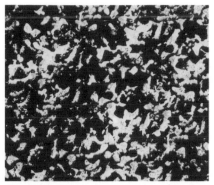

⊕ Pink

⊕ Purple

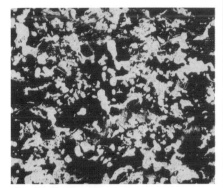

⊕ Light gray

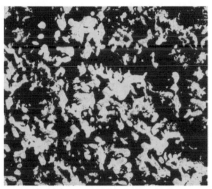

⊕ Peach

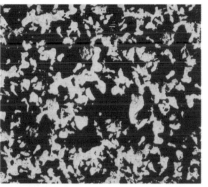

⊕ Buff

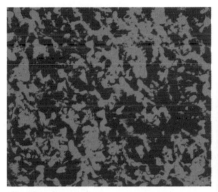

⊕ Dark gray

Ⓘ Crimson red

⊕ Terracotta

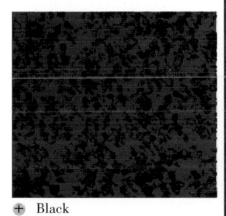

⊕ Black

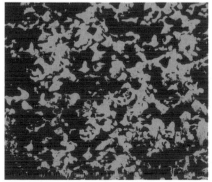

⊕ Lilac

⊕ Brown

⊕ White

Dragging

Spattering

+ Dark yellow

+ Purple

+ Dark yellow and red

+ Purple and lilac

+ Dark yellow, red and peach

+ Purple , lilac and dark blue

Stippling

Combing

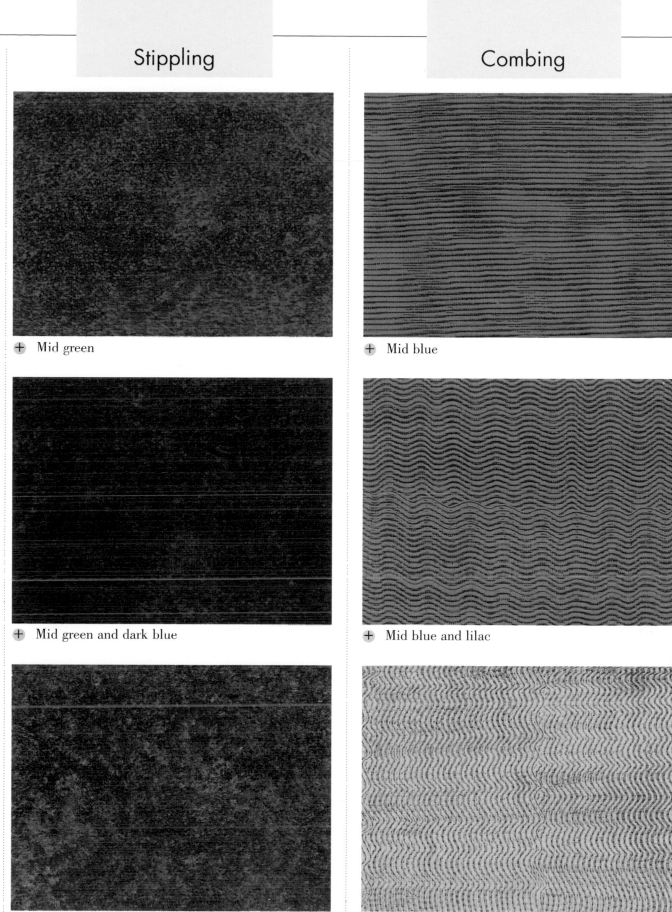

+ Mid green

+ Mid blue

+ Mid green and dark blue

+ Mid blue and lilac

+ Mid green, dark blue and dark yellow

+ Mid blue, lilac and pink

115

Color Washing

Stencilling

+ Crimson red

+ White

+ Crimson red and purple

+ White and dark yellow

+ Crimson red, purple and dark blue

+ White, dark yellow and dark green

Frottage

Rag Rolling

+ Red

+ Turquoise

+ Red and bright orange

+ Turquoise and mid blue

+ Red, bright orange and dark yellow

+ Turquoise, mid blue and red

117

Sponging

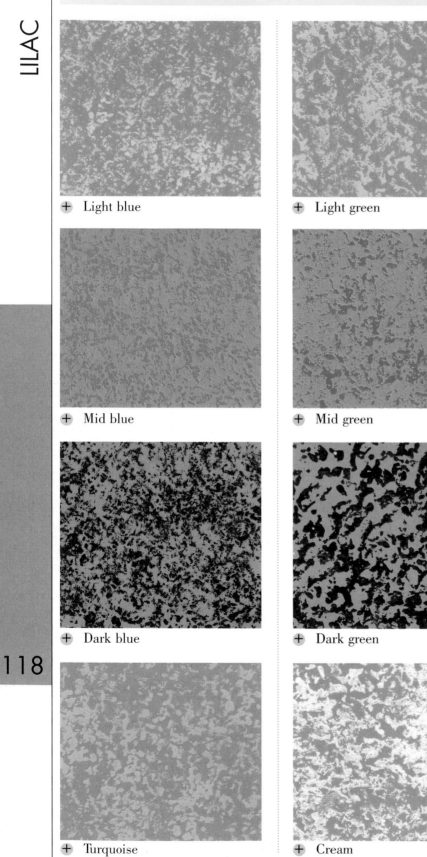

+ Light blue

+ Light green

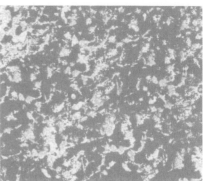

+ Lemon yellow

+ Mid blue

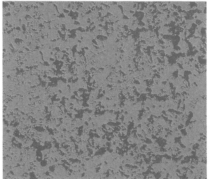

+ Mid green

+ Dark yellow

+ Dark blue

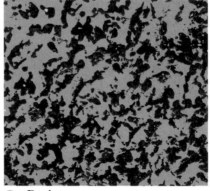

+ Dark green

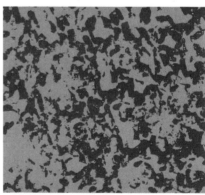

+ Bright orange

+ Turquoise

+ Cream

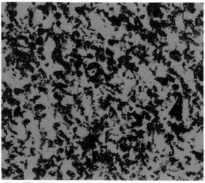

+ Red

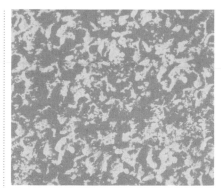

+ Pink

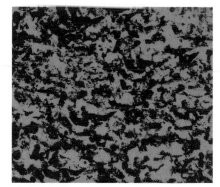

+ Purple

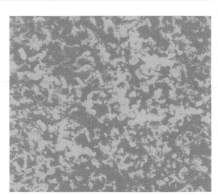

+ Light gray

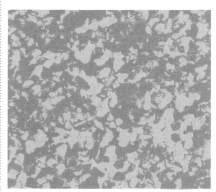

+ Peach

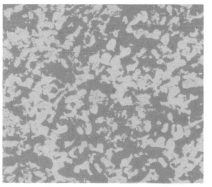

+ Buff

+ Dark gray

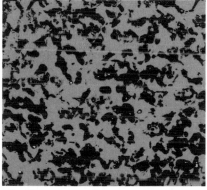

+ Crimson red

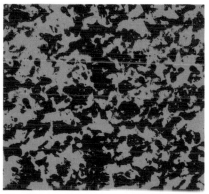

+ Terracotta

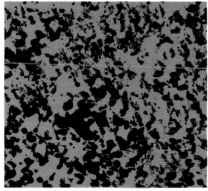

+ Black

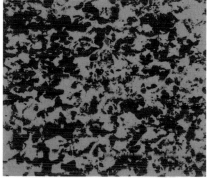

+ Burgundy

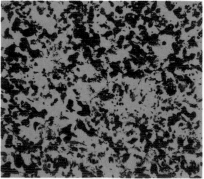

+ Brown

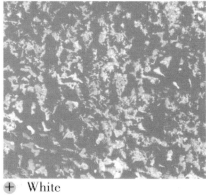

+ White

119

Dragging

Spattering

+ Purple

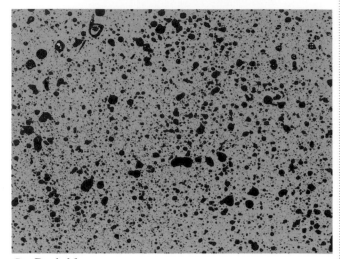

+ Dark blue

+ Purple and dark blue

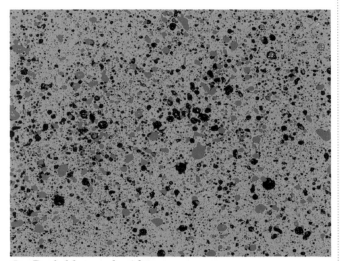

+ Dark blue and mid green

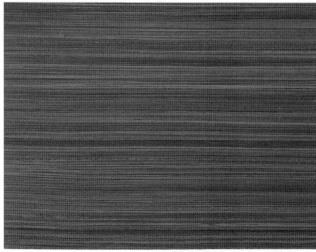

+ Purple, dark blue and mid blue

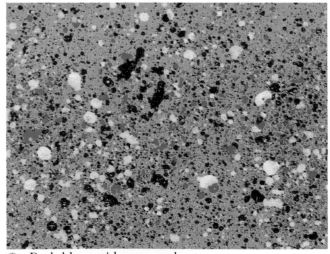

+ Dark blue, mid green and cream

Stippling

Peach

Peach and light gray

Peach, light gray and light green

Combing

Dark gray

Dark gray and light gray

Dark gray, light gray and turquoise

121

Color Washing

Stencilling

✛ Dark blue

✛ Light green

✛ Dark blue and light blue

✛ Light green and turquoise

✛ Dark blue, light blue and lemon yellow

✛ Light green, turquoise and mid blue

Frottage

⊕ Crimson red

⊕ Crimson red and dark green

⊕ Crimson red, dark green and mid green

Rag Rolling

⊕ Light blue

⊕ Light blue and mid blue

⊕ Light blue, mid blue and buff

Sponging

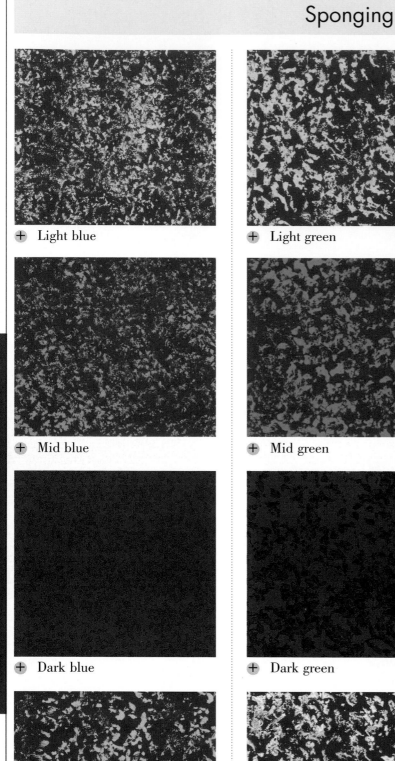

+ Light blue

+ Mid blue

+ Dark blue

+ Turquoise

+ Light green

+ Mid green

+ Dark green

+ Cream

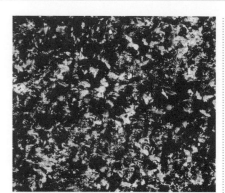

+ Lemon yellow

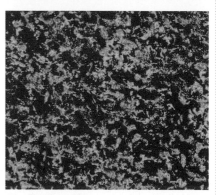

+ Dark yellow

+ Bright orange

+ Red

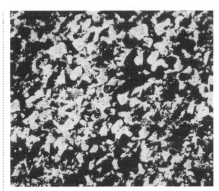

+ Pink

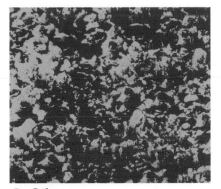

+ Lilac

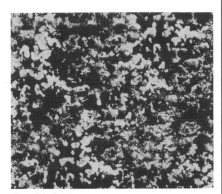

+ Light gray

+ Peach

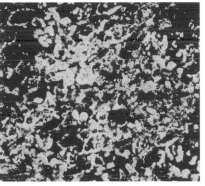

+ Buff

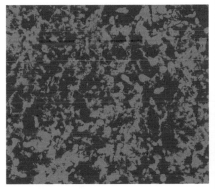

+ Dark gray

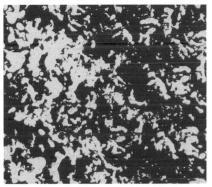

+ Crimson red

+ Terracotta

+ Black

+ Burgundy

+ Brown

+ White

125

PURPLE

Dragging

Spattering

+ Mid blue

+ Red

+ Mid blue and light blue

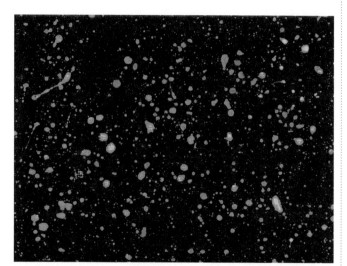

+ Red and dark yellow

+ Mid blue, light blue and lilac

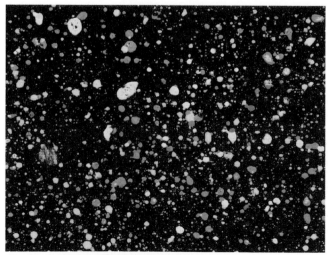

+ Red, dark yellow and cream

Stippling

Combing

⊕ Crimson red

⊕ Dark blue

⊕ Crimson red and burgundy

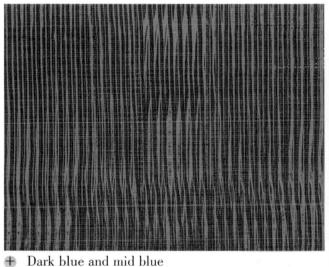

⊕ Dark blue and mid blue

⊕ Crimson red, burgundy and dark blue

⊕ Dark blue, mid blue and red

127

Color Washing

Stencilling

➕ Mid blue

➕ Peach

➕ Mid blue and mid green

➕ Peach and turquoise

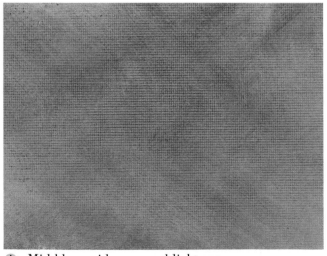

➕ Mid blue, mid green and light gray

➕ Peach, turquoise and crimson red

Frottage

Rag Rolling

+ Mid green

+ Lilac

+ Mid green and peach

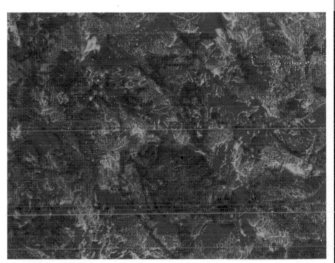

+ Lilac and burgundy

+ Mid green, peach and crimson red

+ Lilac, burgundy and bright orange

Sponging

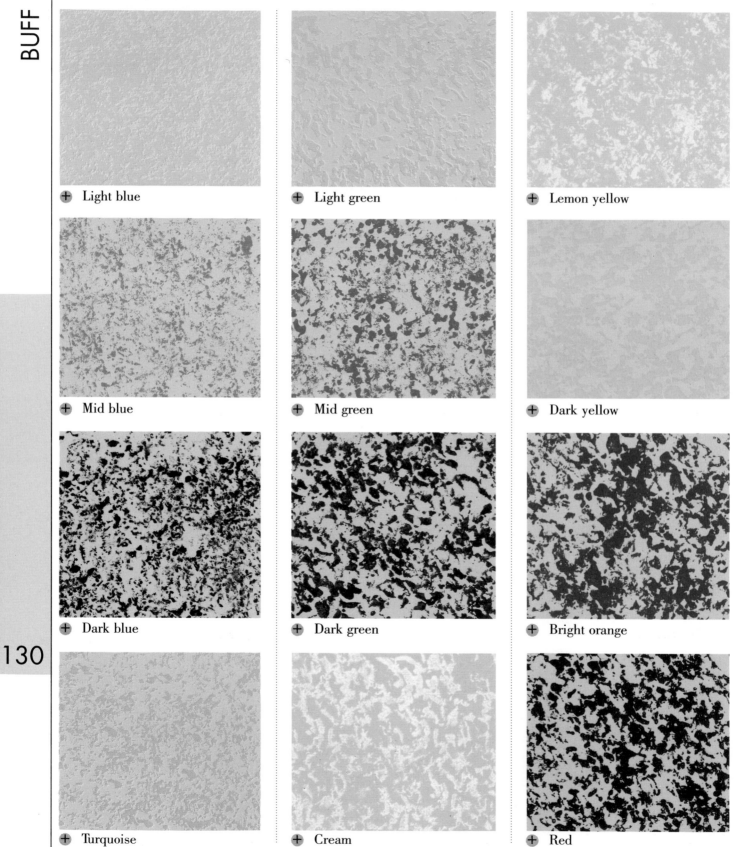

+ Light blue

+ Light green

+ Lemon yellow

+ Mid blue

+ Mid green

+ Dark yellow

+ Dark blue

+ Dark green

+ Bright orange

+ Turquoise

+ Cream

+ Red

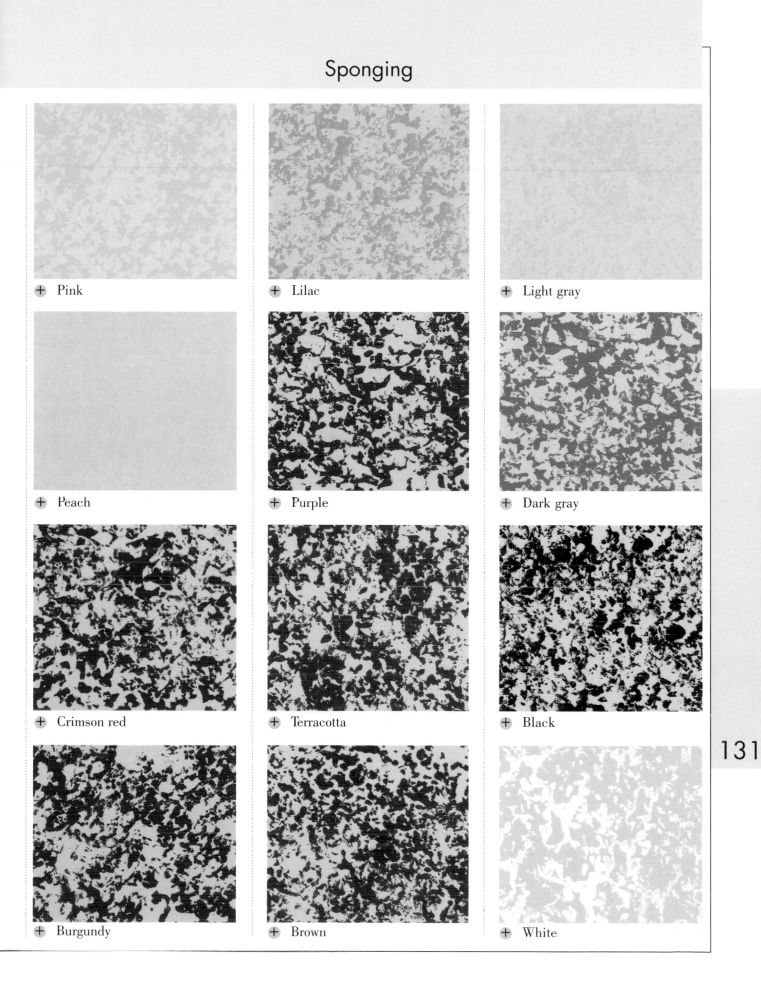

+ Pink

+ Lilac

+ Light gray

+ Peach

+ Purple

+ Dark gray

+ Crimson red

+ Terracotta

+ Black

+ Burgundy

+ Brown

+ White

Dragging

⊕ Dark yellow

⊕ Dark yellow and mid green

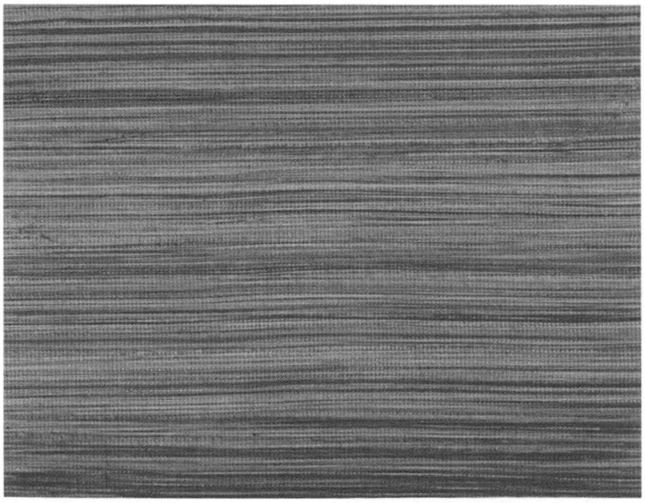

⊕ Dark yellow, mid green and bright orange

Spattering

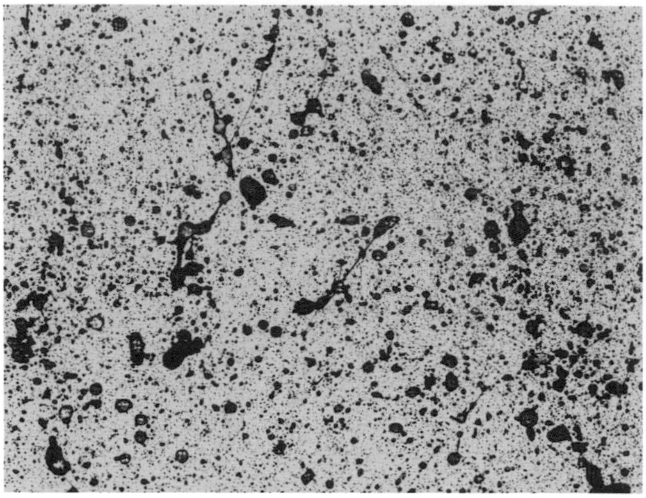

⊕ Red

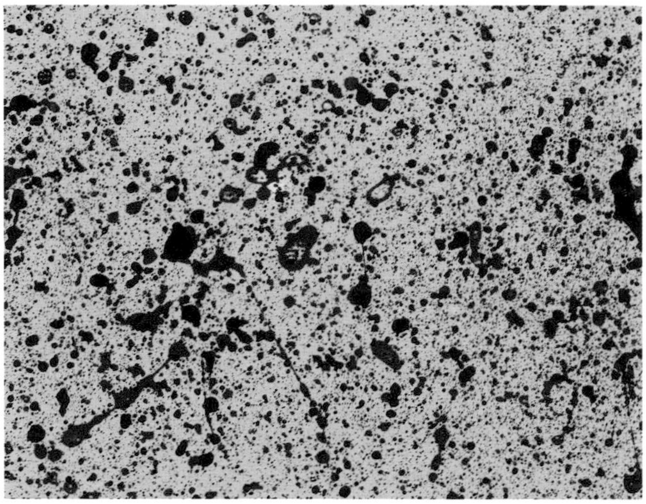

⊕ Red and dark blue

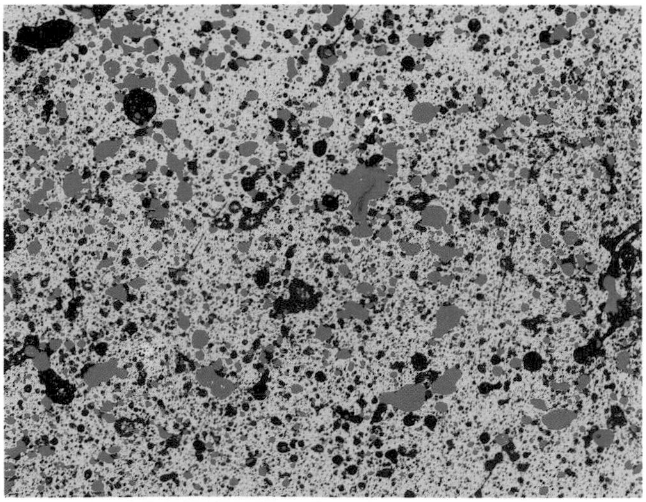

⊕ Red, dark blue and mid green

Stippling

✛ Lilac

✛ Lilac and purple

✛ Lilac, purple and pink

Combing

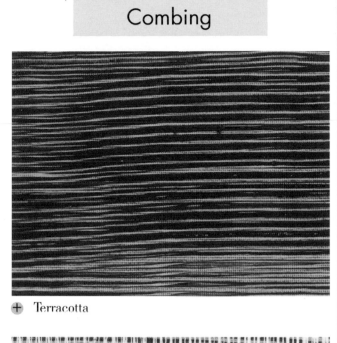

✛ Terracotta

✛ Terracotta and lemon yellow

✛ Terracotta, lemon yellow and bright orange

133

Color Washing

Stencilling

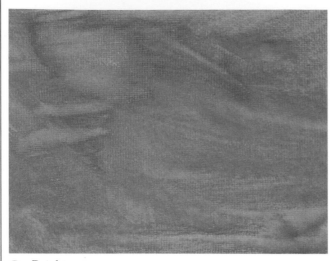

+ Bright orange

+ Light green

+ Bright orange and dark yellow

+ Light green and dark yellow

+ Bright orange, dark yellow and burgundy

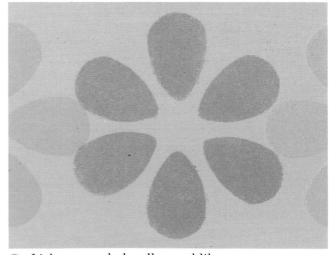

+ Light green, dark yellow and lilac

Frottage

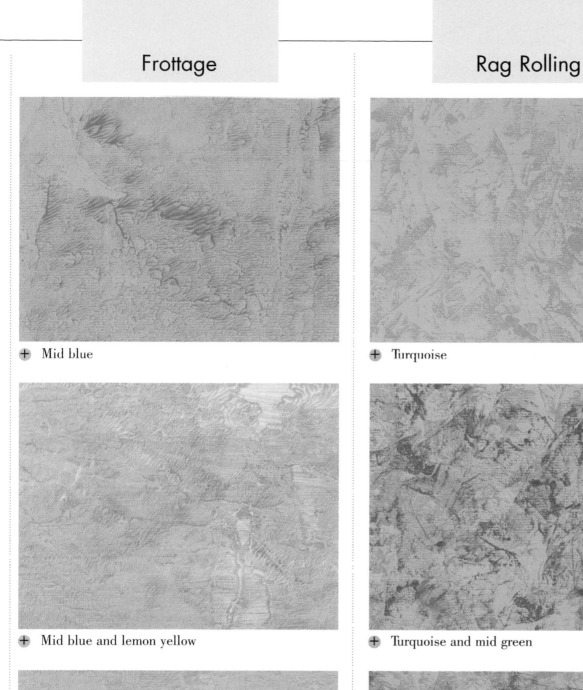

⊕ Mid blue

⊕ Mid blue and lemon yellow

⊕ Mid blue, lemon yellow and light gray

Rag Rolling

⊕ Turquoise

⊕ Turquoise and mid green

⊕ Turquoise, mid green and dark yellow

Sponging

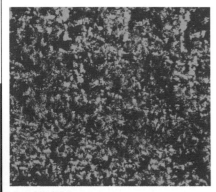

+ Light blue

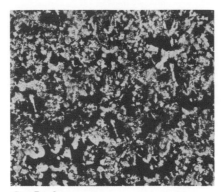

+ Light green

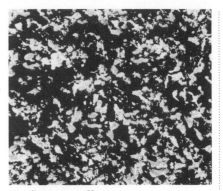

+ Lemon yellow

+ Mid blue

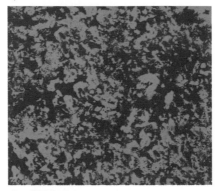

+ Mid green

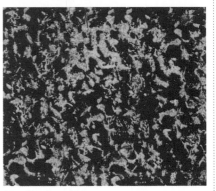

+ Dark yellow

+ Dark blue

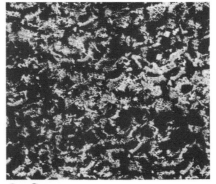

+ Dark green

+ Bright orange

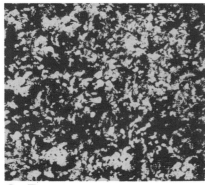

+ Turquoise

+ Cream

+ Red

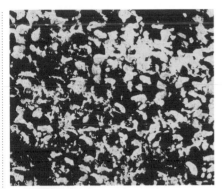

+ Pink

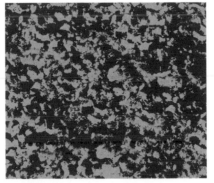

+ Lilac

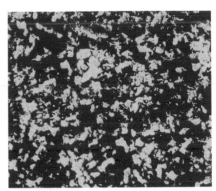

+ Light gray

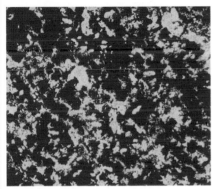

+ Peach

+ Purple

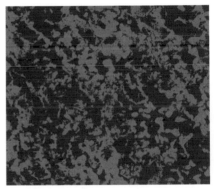

+ Dark gray

+ Crimson red

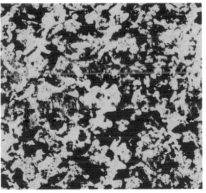

+ Buff

+ Black

137

+ Burgundy

+ Brown

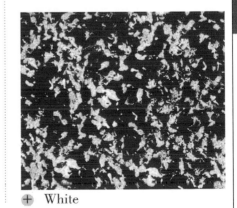

+ White

TERRACOTTA

Dragging

Spattering

+ Buff

+ Turquoise

+ Buff and dark gray

+ Turquoise and crimson red

+ Buff, dark gray and dark blue

+ Turquoise, crimson red and peach

Stippling

+ Lemon yellow

+ Lemon yellow and dark yellow

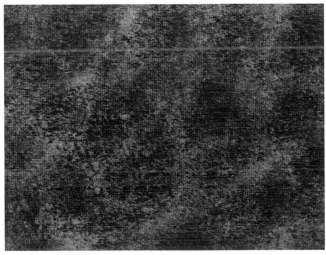

+ Lemon yellow, dark yellow and crimson red

Combing

+ Red

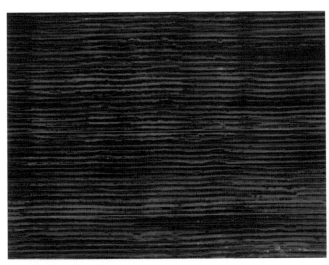

+ Red and mid green

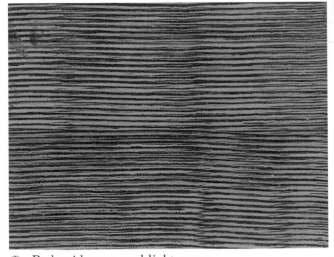

+ Red, mid green and light green

139

Color Washing

Stencilling

+ Peach

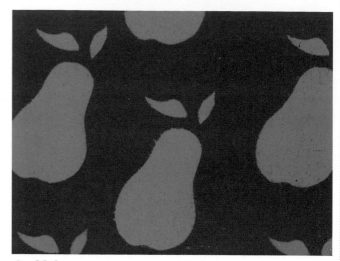

+ Mid green

+ Peach and turquoise

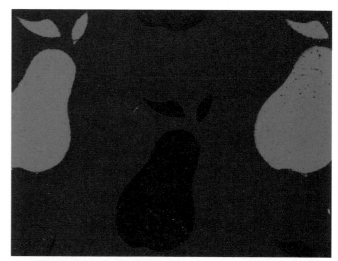

+ Mid green and dark green

+ Peach, turquoise and mid green

+ Mid green, dark green and bright orange

Frottage

Rag Rolling

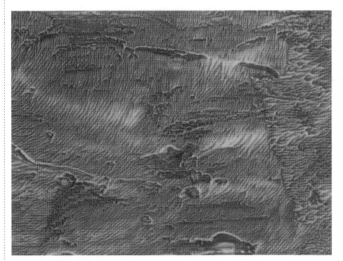

⊕ Dark yellow

⊕ Turquoise

⊕ Dark yellow and red

⊕ Turquoise and mid blue

⊕ Dark yellow, red and buff

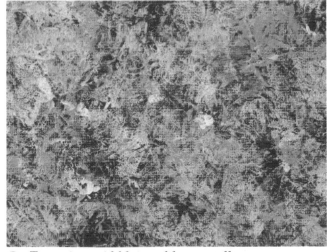

⊕ Turquoise, mid blue and lemon yellow

BROWN

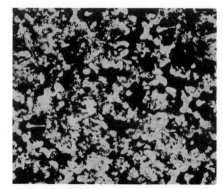

⊕ Light blue

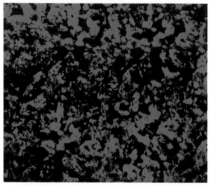

⊕ Light green

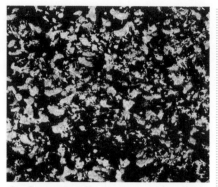

⊕ Lemon yellow

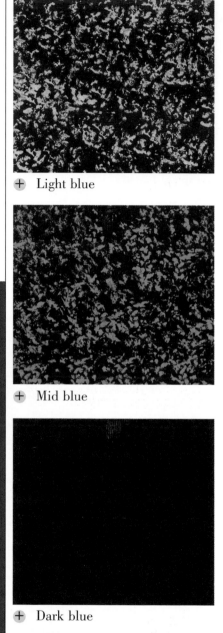

⊕ Mid blue

⊕ Mid green

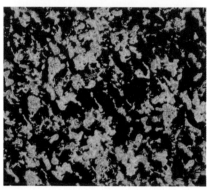

⊕ Dark yellow

⊕ Dark blue

⊕ Dark green

⊕ Bright orange

142

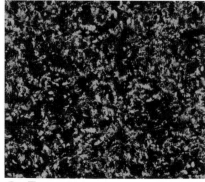

⊕ Turquoise

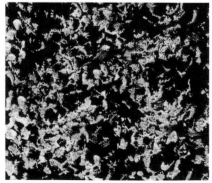

⊕ Cream

⊕ Red

+ Pink

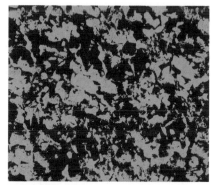

+ Lilac

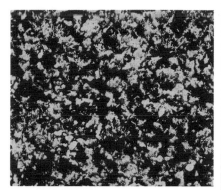

+ Light gray

+ Peach

+ Purple

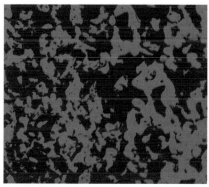

+ Dark gray

+ Crimson red

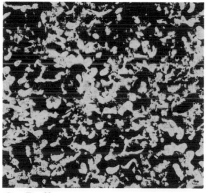

+ Buff

+ Black

+ Burgundy

 Terracotta

 White

Dragging

Spattering

+ Mid blue

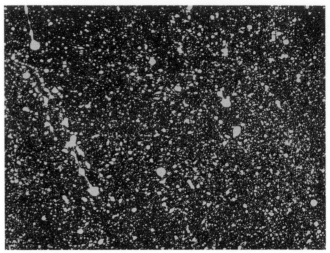

+ Peach

+ Mid blue and mid green

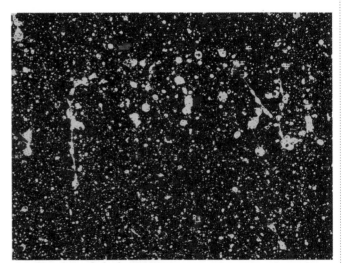

+ Peach and dark green

144

+ Mid blue, mid green and lilac

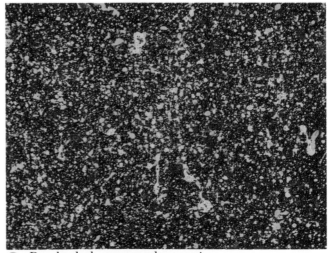

+ Peach, dark green and turquoise

Stippling

Combing

+ Peach

+ Mid green

+ Peach and bright orange

+ Mid green and light green

+ Peach, bright orange and mid green

+ Mid green, light green and lilac

145

Color Washing

Stencilling

+ Terracotta

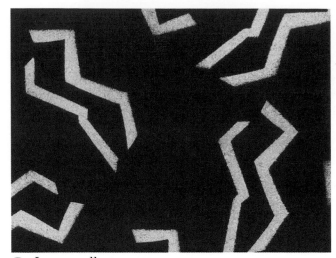

+ Lemon yellow

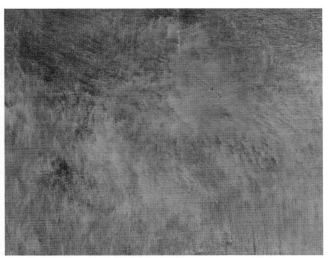

+ Terracotta and dark yellow

+ Lemon yellow and dark yellow

+ Terracotta, dark yellow and bright orange

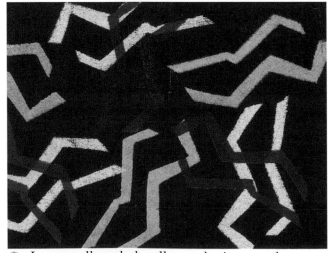

+ Lemon yellow, dark yellow and crimson red

Frottage

Rag Rolling

⊕ Light blue

⊕ Dark gray

⊕ Light blue and mid green

⊕ Dark gray and black

⊕ Light blue, mid green and bright orange

⊕ Dark gray, black and buff

Sponging

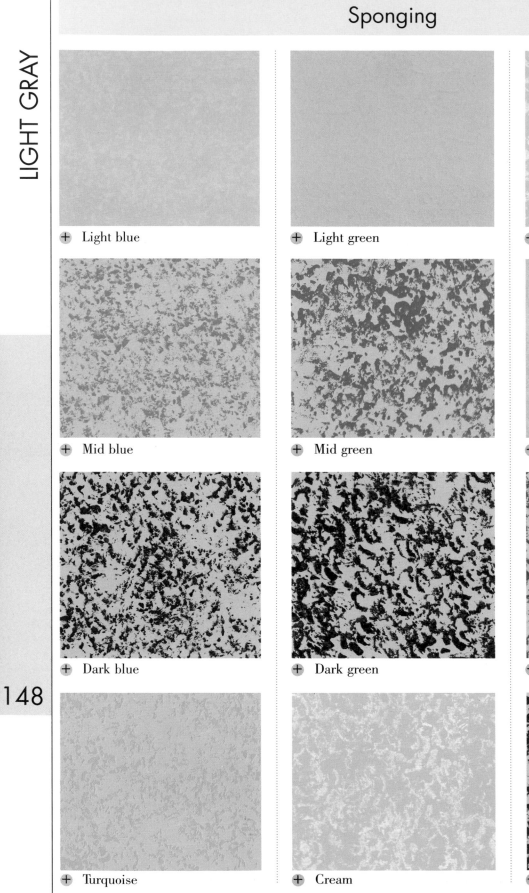

+ Light blue

+ Light green

+ Lemon yellow

+ Mid blue

+ Mid green

+ Dark yellow

+ Dark blue

+ Dark green

+ Bright orange

+ Turquoise

+ Cream

+ Red

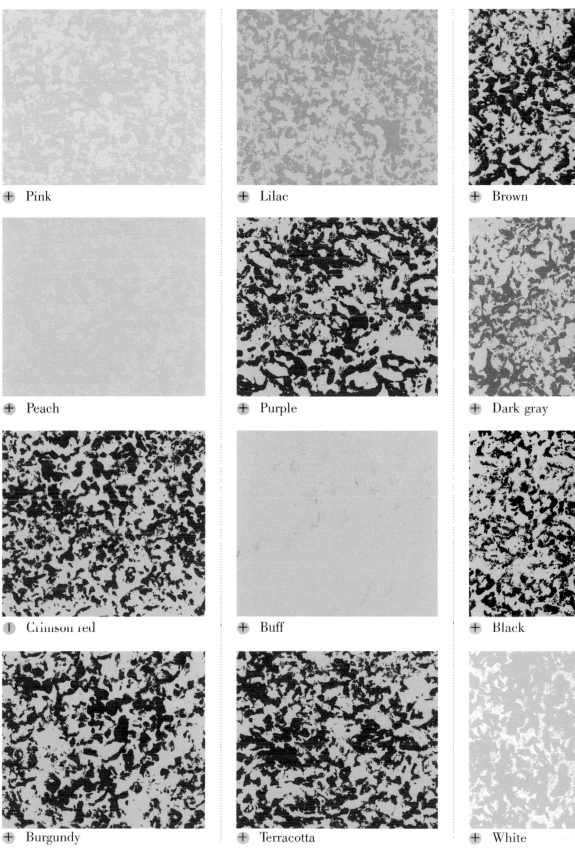

+ Pink

+ Lilac

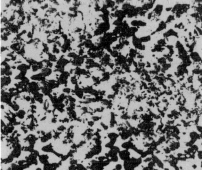

+ Brown

+ Peach

+ Purple

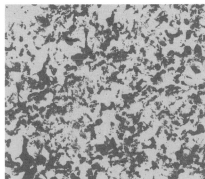

+ Dark gray

① Crimson red

+ Buff

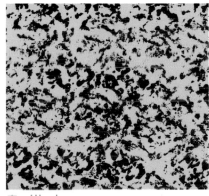

+ Black

+ Burgundy

+ Terracotta

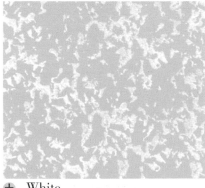

+ White

Dragging

Spattering

+ Dark yellow

+ Peach

+ Dark yellow and dark blue

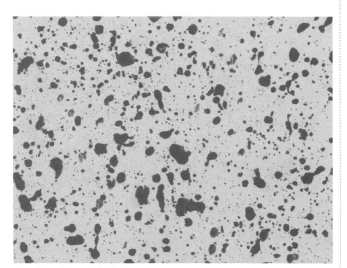

+ Peach and bright orange

+ Dark yellow, dark blue and light green

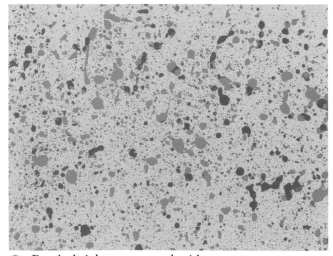

+ Peach, bright orange and mid green

150

Stippling

Combing

+ Light green

+ Lilac

+ Light green and lemon yellow

+ Lilac and turquoise

+ Light green, lemon yellow and dark yellow

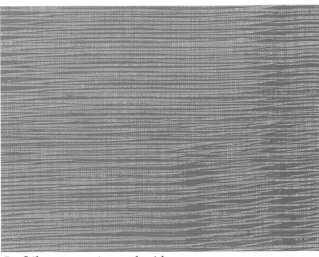

+ Lilac, turquoise and mid green

151

Color Washing

Stencilling

+ Dark blue

+ Mid blue

+ Dark blue and dark yellow

+ Mid blue and lemon yellow

+ Dark blue, dark yellow and red

+ Mid blue, lemon yellow and peach

Frottage

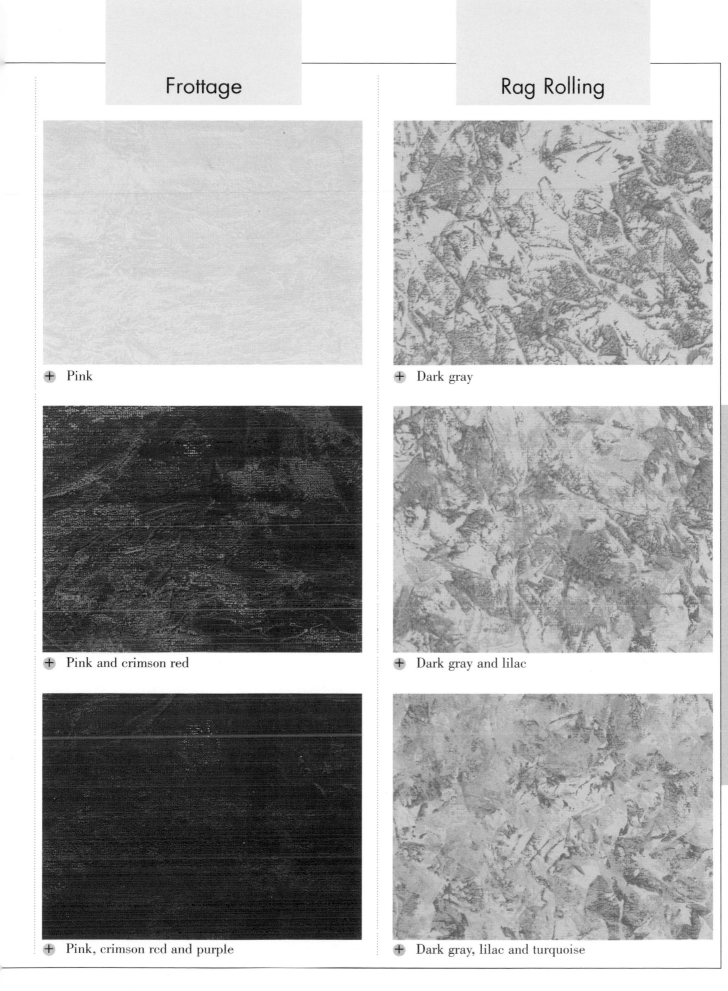

+ Pink

+ Pink and crimson red

+ Pink, crimson red and purple

Rag Rolling

+ Dark gray

+ Dark gray and lilac

+ Dark gray, lilac and turquoise

153

Sponging

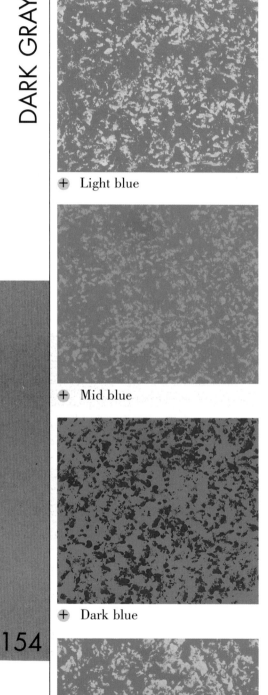

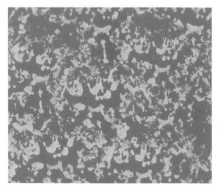

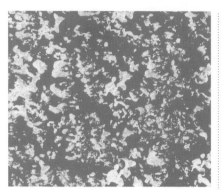

+ Light blue

+ Light green

+ Lemon yellow

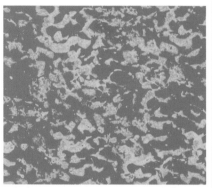

+ Mid blue

+ Mid green

+ Dark yellow

+ Dark blue

+ Dark green

+ Bright orange

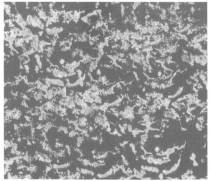

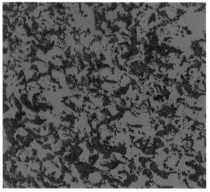

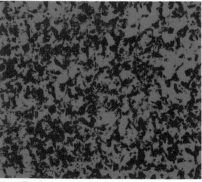

+ Turquoise

+ Cream

 Red

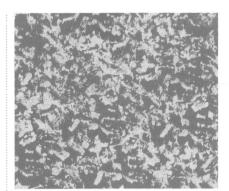

+ Pink

+ Lilac

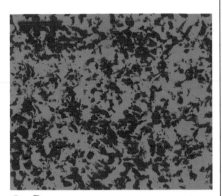

+ Brown

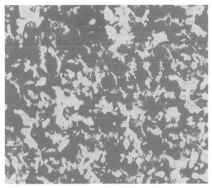

+ Peach

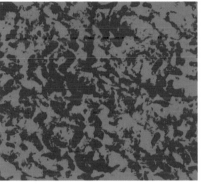

+ Purple

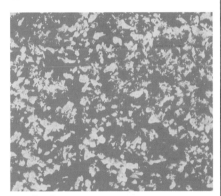

+ Light gray

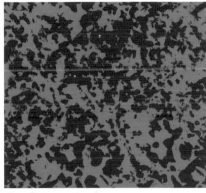

+ Crimson red

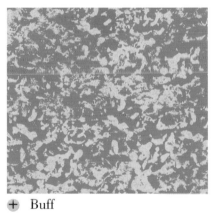

+ Buff

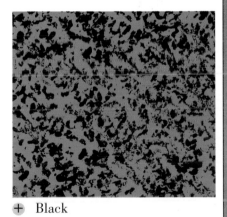

+ Black

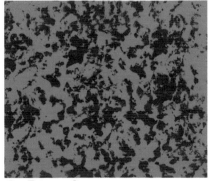

+ Burgundy

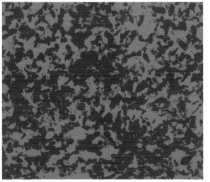

+ Terracotta

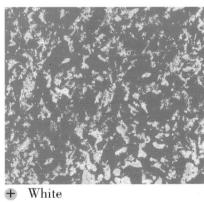

+ White

155

Dragging

Spattering

+ Lilac

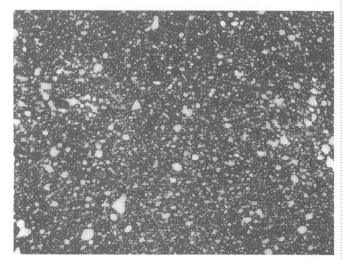

+ White

+ Lilac and purple

+ White and black

+ Lilac, purple and mid blue

+ White, black and turquoise

Stippling

Combing

✛ Dark yellow

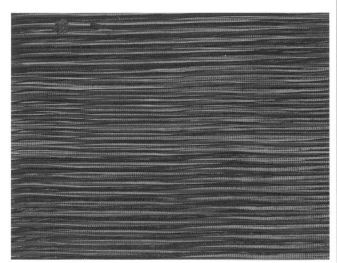

✛ Buff

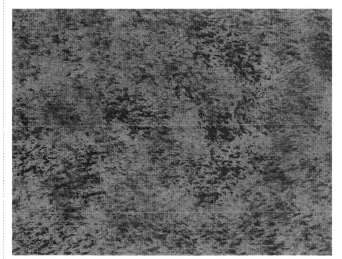

✛ Dark yellow and dark blue

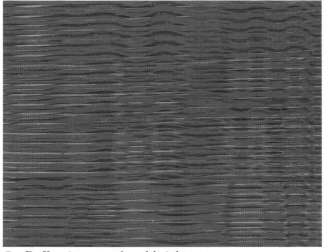

✛ Buff and crimson red

✛ Dark yellow, dark blue and mid blue

✛ Buff, crimson red and bright orange

Color Washing

Stencilling

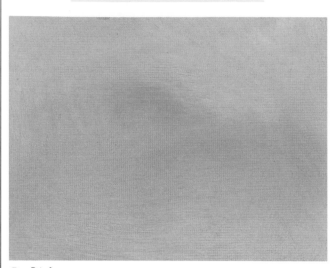

⊕ Light green

⊕ Mid blue

⊕ Light green and mid green

⊕ Mid blue and lilac

⊕ Light green, mid green and red

⊕ Mid blue, lilac and dark green

Frottage

Rag Rolling

+ Purple

+ Red

+ Purple and lilac

+ Red and dark yellow

+ Purple, lilac and turquoise

+ Red, dark yellow and mid blue

BLACK

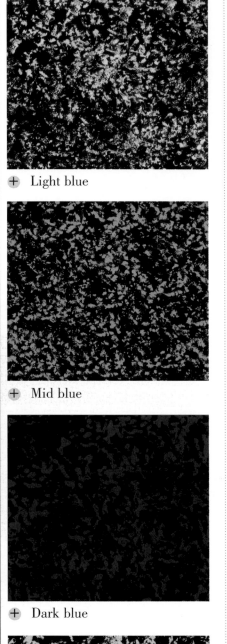

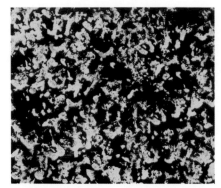

+ Light blue

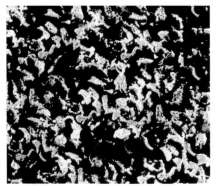

+ Light green

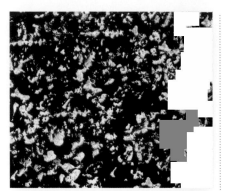

+ Lemon yellow

+ Mid blue

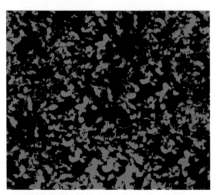

+ Mid green

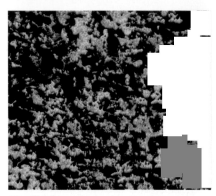

+ Dark yellow

+ Dark blue

+ Dark green

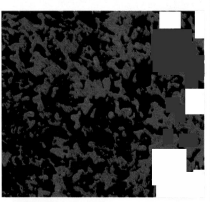

+ Bright orange

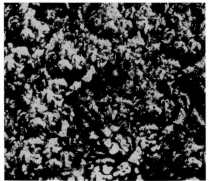

+ Turquoise

+ Cream

+ Red

+ Pink	+ Lilac	+ Brown
+ Peach	+ Purple	+ Light gray
+ Crimson red	+ Buff	+ Dark gray
+ Burgundy	+ Terracotta	+ White

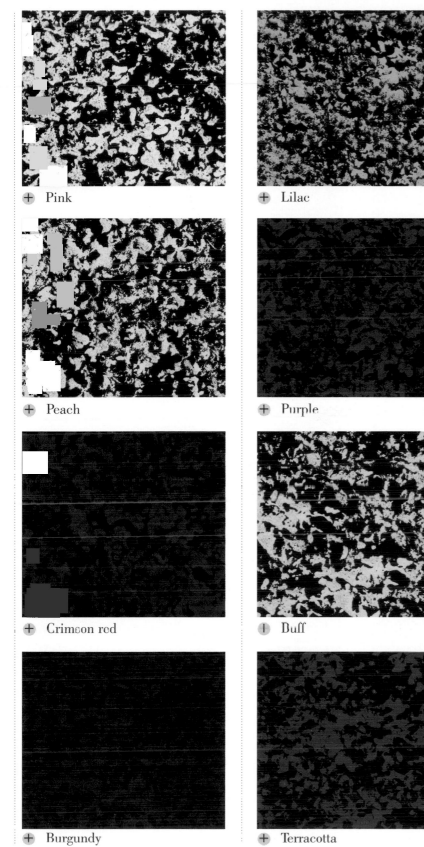
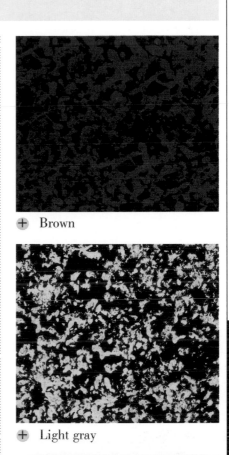
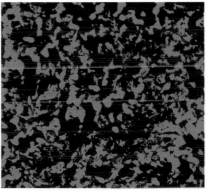

Dragging

Spattering

+ Mid blue

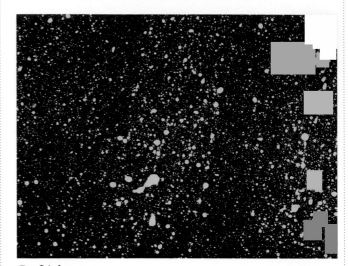

+ Light green

+ Mid blue and purple

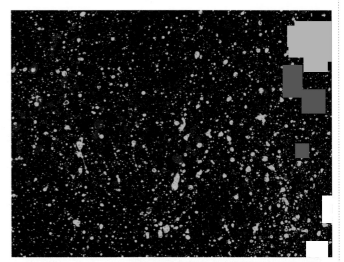

+ Light green and crimson red

+ Mid blue, purple and light blue

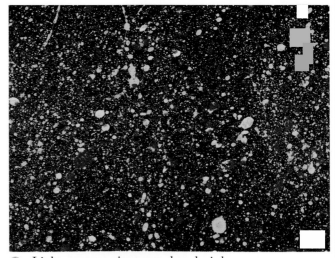

+ Light green, crimson red and pink

Stippling

+ Burgundy

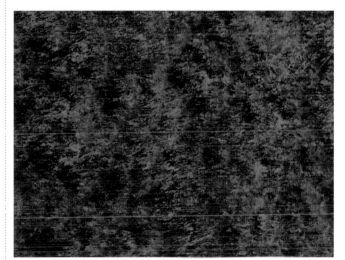

+ Burgundy and mid green

+ Burgundy, mid green and turquoise

Combing

+ Purple

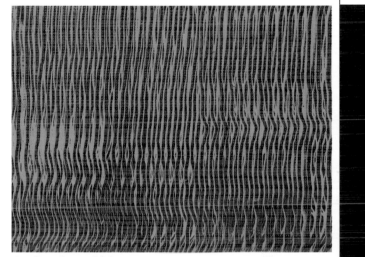

+ Purple and lilac

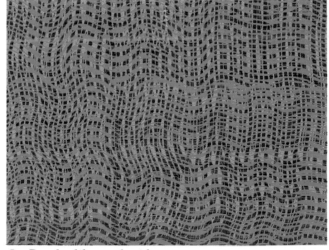

+ Purple, lilac and mid green

Color Washing

Stencilling

+ Mid blue

+ Crimson red

+ Mid blue and dark blue

+ Crimson red and dark blue

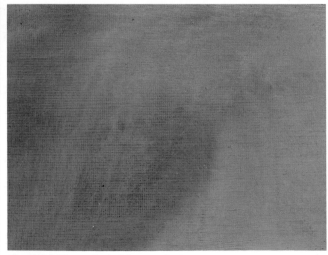

+ Mid blue, dark blue and cream

+ Crimson red, dark blue and purple

Frottage

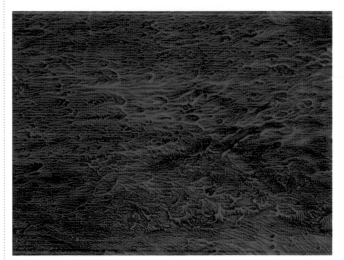

✛ Bright orange

✛ Bright orange and dark yellow

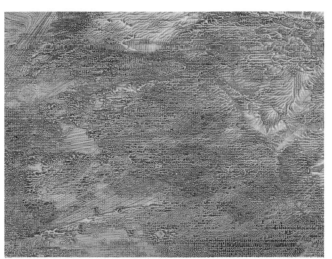

✛ Bright orange, dark yellow and cream

Rag Rolling

✛ White

✛ White and dark gray

✛ White, dark gray and purple

Sponging

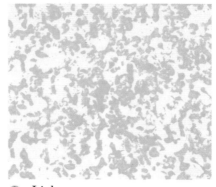

+ Light blue

+ Light green

+ Lemon yellow

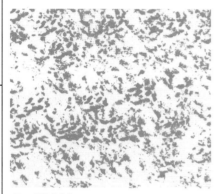

+ Mid blue

+ Mid green

+ Dark yellow

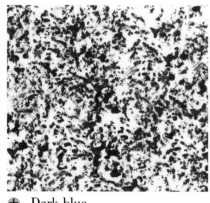

+ Dark blue

+ Dark green

+ Bright orange

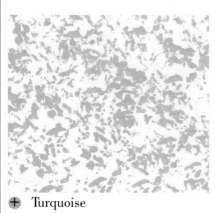

+ Turquoise

+ Cream

+ Red

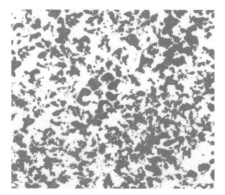

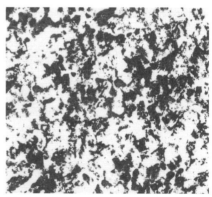
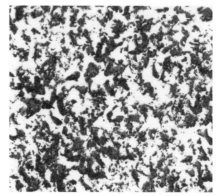

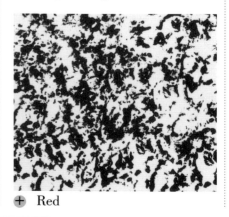

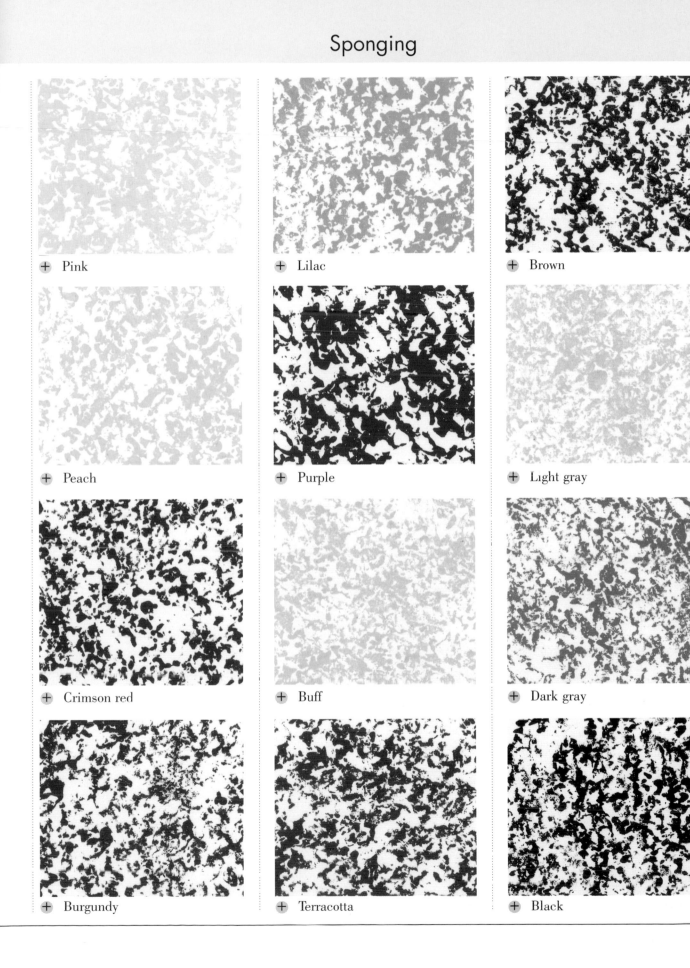

+ Pink

+ Lilac

+ Brown

+ Peach

+ Purple

+ Light gray

+ Crimson red

+ Buff

+ Dark gray

+ Burgundy

+ Terracotta

+ Black

Dragging

Spattering

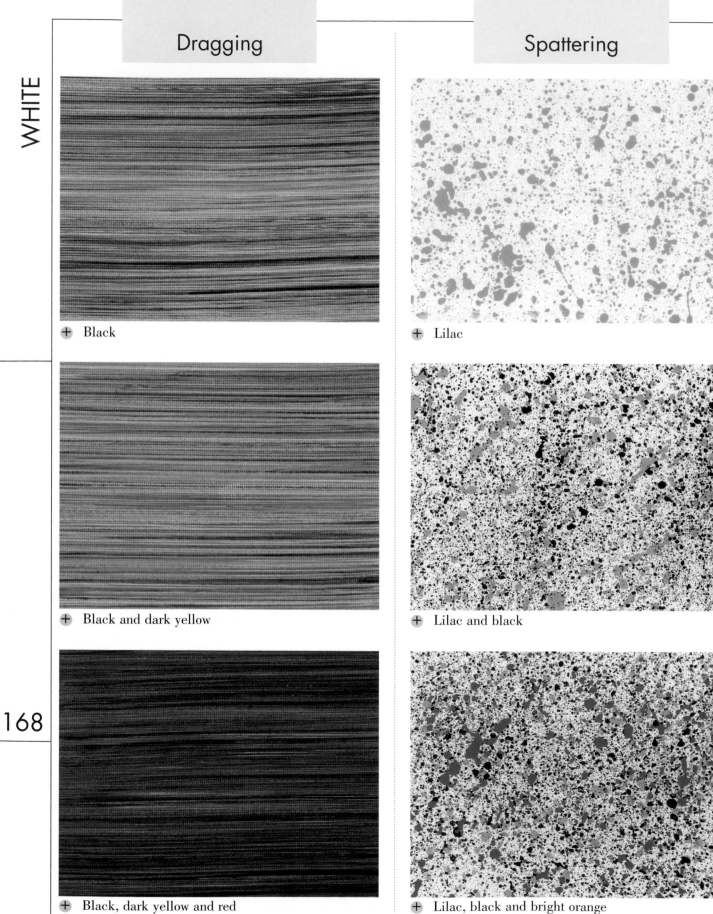

+ Black

+ Lilac

+ Black and dark yellow

+ Lilac and black

+ Black, dark yellow and red

+ Lilac, black and bright orange

Stippling

+ Turquoise

+ Turquoise and peach

+ Turquoise, peach and pink

Combing

+ Dark green

+ Dark green and dark blue

+ Dark green, dark blue and dark yellow

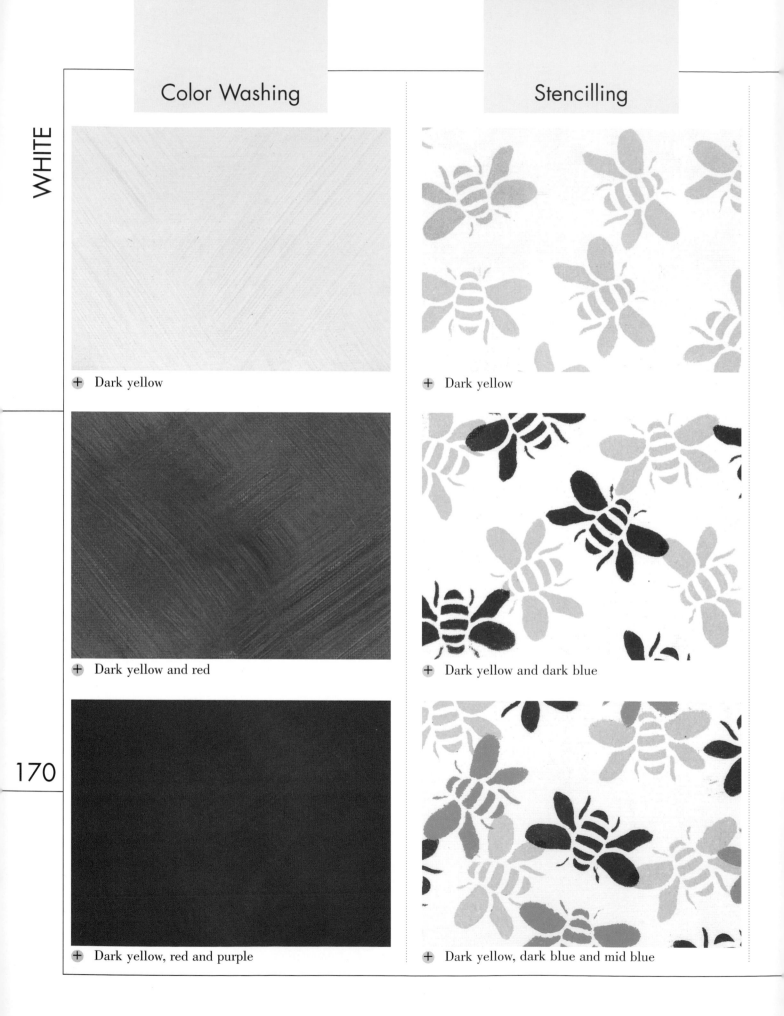

Color Washing

Stencilling

+ Dark yellow

+ Dark yellow

+ Dark yellow and red

+ Dark yellow and dark blue

+ Dark yellow, red and purple

+ Dark yellow, dark blue and mid blue

Frottage

Rag Rolling

⊕ Light blue

⊕ Bright orange

⊕ Light blue and pink

⊕ Bright orange and peach

⊕ Light blue, pink and lilac

⊕ Bright orange, peach and red

Introduction

Since the beginning of the human race, people have attempted to create images of the outside world on the walls of their homes, drawing from a vast and sometimes threatening environment aspects that are beautiful, enjoyable and help remove the stresses of everyday life.

Paint is a universally available, inexpensive and simple way of enhancing and protecting the very fabric of our homes. It is also a powerful and magical medium. This book demonstrates how to achieve many interesting and versatile broken-color effects. But these are only the beginning. Down through the centuries, marbles and gemstones, precious woods and rare and costly fabrics have been lovingly recreated in paint, becoming available even to those in the humblest abodes.

Starry nights, moiré silk walls, granite columns astride secret gardens and Roman mosaic bathrooms are just a few of the special effects that you could soon be producing with relative ease. The following pages simplify these and other truly individual techniques to bring them within the reach of everyone from the novice decorator to the professional interior designer. By following the step-by-step instructions, you could soon enjoy the beauty of lapis lazuli, the warmth of tarnished pewter or the charm of the antique in your home.

1 Paint the surface with two coats of vinyl semigloss (silk) latex (emulsion), allowing drying time between each coat.

2 Carefully load a flexible-bristled brush with paint of your chosen top color, and remove the excess. Drag lightly across the ground surface.

3 Stencil and line if you wish. Seal with an acrylic varnish if extra protection is needed.

1 After preparing your surface, apply two coats of vinyl semigloss (silk) latex (emulsion), allowing drying time between coats. Dry the final coat overnight.

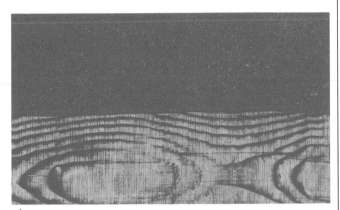

4 Drag a rocker through the glaze to produce the characteristic wood-grain look. Allow glaze to go tacky.

2 Mix your chosen top-coat color – in this case, pale coffee – with an acrylic glazing medium, following manufacturer's instructions. Paint onto base coat.

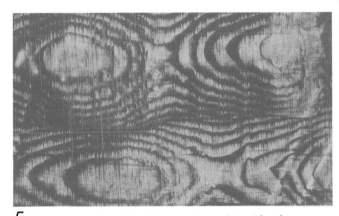

5 Gently cross-drag (drag across the grain) with a long-haired dragging brush, over the entire surface.

3 Carefully and fully stipple out all brushstrokes to create an even finish.

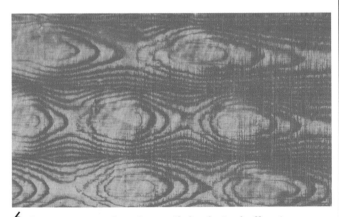

6 Continue cross-dragging until the desired effect is achieved. Finish with a coat of acrylic varnish.

Granite

Craquelure

1 Paint two coats of pale gray onto the surface, leaving to dry between coats. Check that the second coat is thoroughly dry before proceeding.

1 Paint your surface with a base coat of your chosen color. When it is thoroughly dry, apply a second coat. Leave to dry. Stencil if you have chosen to do so, and again allow to dry.

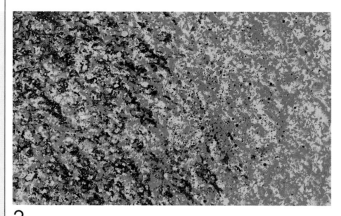

2 Sponge over with dark gray, followed by black, and then white. Alow each layer to dry before applying the next.

2 Apply a liberal coat of craquelure base coat. Allow to dry. Overpaint with the craquelure top coat in random directions. As this coat dries, a web of fine cracks will appear. Crackle varnish produces the same effect. Dry completely.

3 Stencil and line in black to create the appearance of inlaid granite. After drying, protect with two coats of suitable gloss varnish.

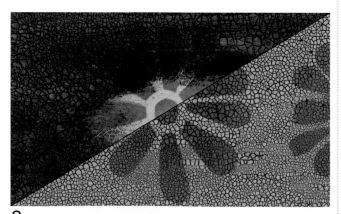

3 Rub some artists' oil paint into the surface with a soft cloth. We chose raw umber to give an antique effect. Remove excess paint immediately, leaving the cracks highlighted. Protect with an oil-based varnish.

1 Apply two coats of black eggshell to your prepared surface, allowing each to dry overnight.

2 Mix an oil glaze or gilp (see pages 16 and 189), or use a store-bought transparent oil glaze. Remove dust from your base coat with a little linseed oil, and paint on the glaze.

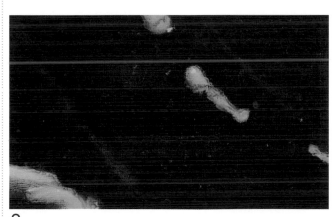

3 Place separately on a dish small amounts of viridian and white artists' oil paint. Mix each with a little glaze, and dab across the surface.

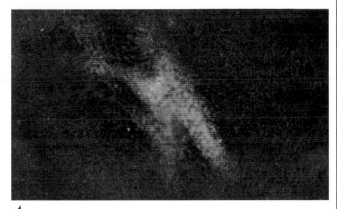

4 Stipple out with a good stippling brush, and soften with either a badger softener or a soft dusting brush.

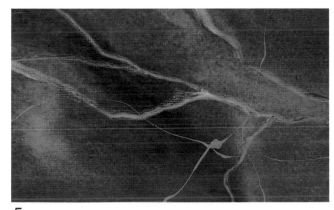

5 Add veins in white with a fine sable brush, and very carefully soften the edges again. Add some more veins in gold if you wish.

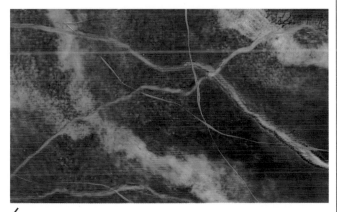

6 When you have achieved an aesthetically pleasing effect, apply at least three coats of gloss varnish. Carefully wet-and-dry sand the surface between coats.

Lapis lazuli

1 Paint your surface with at least two coats of mid to strong blue eggshell, and allow to dry.

4 Carefully diffuse the effect with a random sponging of white artists' oil paint. A tiny amount of ocher yellow can be used to create veins.

2 Over-sponge the surface with a little French ultramarine artists' oil paint mixed with transparent oil glaze or gilp (see pages 16 and 189).

5 Spatter a little gold powder onto the wet ground, and allow to dry completely.

3 While this is still wet, sponge another layer over it in Prussian blue artists' oil color.

6 Line and decorate as required, using a gilding wax. Seal with two coats of polyurethane spray varnish.

Verdigris

1 Paint onto your surface two coats of water-based gold acrylic paint, and allow to dry. Dab onto the base coat patches of bright green, white and a little aquamarine blue.

2 Using a stippling brush, gently stipple the three colors together to create that typical verdigris patina.

3 While the paint is still a little wet, remove some areas with a lint-free cloth, allowing parts of the gold base coat to show through. Coat with acrylic varnish if necessary.

Crackle glaze

1 Paint your surface with two coats of flat latex (emulsion), drying thoroughly between coats. This will be the color of the cracks.

2 Paint on a liberal layer of crackle glaze suitable for use with latex (emulsion) paint, using randomly directional brushstrokes. Allow to dry. The glaze will cause the following layer of paint to crack, so that the ground shows through.

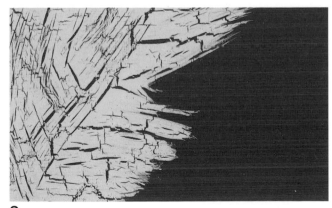

3 Paint on a top coat of contrasting color quickly and evenly. DO NOT OVERBRUSH, because this will disturb the cracking reaction. Leave the effect to dry completely, and seal with wax or varnish.

Wax distressing

Simple wood graining

1 Paint your surface with two coats of your chosen color. This color will be seen through the distressed top coat. Apply some wax polish or candle wax to the base coat where you wish the color to show through. Allow to dry overnight.

1 Apply a base coat of cream or yellow ocher eggshell onto your surface, allow to dry overnight, and repeat. Again, leave to dry overnight.

2 Paint the top coat quickly over the waxed base coat, and leave to dry.

2 Mix some raw sienna oil paint with a little transparent oil glaze or gilp (see p.189), and follow the tinting instructions (see Introduction). Paint onto the base coat, and stipple out the brushstrokes.

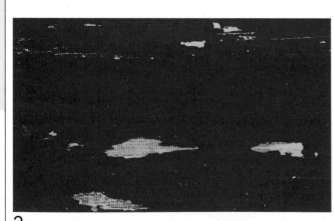

3 Distress the top coat by rubbing with medium to fine sandpaper or fine steel wool, removing all traces of wax in the process. Varnish for protection.

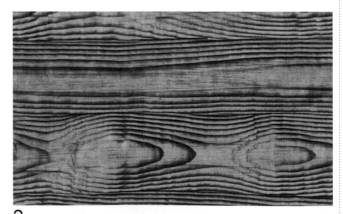

3 Pass a rocker, or heart grainer, through the glaze to achieve the look of heart-grained wood. Rock back and forward as you drag. Varnish for protection.

178

1 Apply two coats of light ocher eggshell to your surface, allowing a drying time of 24 hours between coats.

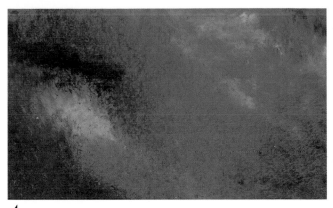

4 Add a little titanium or flake white in squiggles and vein lines, stipple out, and soften as before.

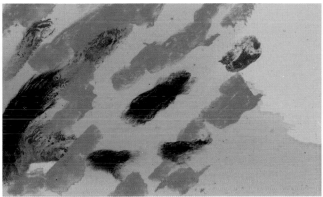

2 Wipe the base coat with a little linseed oil, and apply a fairly liberal film of gilp (see p.189) or transparent oil glaze to the ground. Mix some artists' oils in raw umber, burnt umber, and yellow ocher with a little of the glaze, and squiggle them across the base coat.

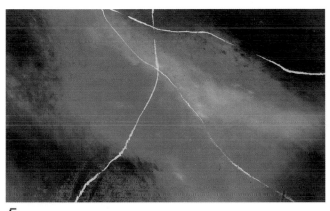

5 Add a few unsoftened veins with a fine brush, if necessary.

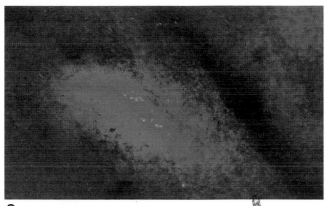

3 Stipple out to an even finish, and soften gently with a good-quality softening brush.

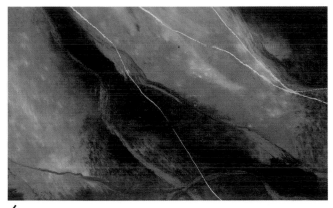

6 Varnish with at least three to four coats of gloss varnish, sanding with wet-and-dry sandpaper between coats.

Simple gilding

1 Apply a base coat of your preferred color. Allow to dry thoroughly, and apply a second coat.

2 Stipple some water-based gold size through a suitable stencil, or hand paint your design in gold size. Allow to go finger-touch dry.

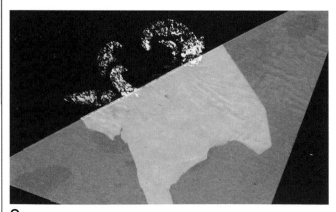

3 Prepare some pieces of gold leaf or Dutch metal, and apply them carefully to the size.

4 Press gently on the transfer paper with a soft cloth to smooth out the leaf or Dutch metal. Allow to dry completely.

5 Remove the backing paper, and carefully brush away the excess with a very soft brush.

6 You can delicately distress the surface, if you wish, with fine steel wool, allowing the base coat to show through. Protect with a gloss varnish.

Malachite

1 Paint your surface with a turquoise eggshell, and allow it to dry overnight. Apply a second coat, and also allow it to dry thoroughly.

2 Mix some transparent oil glaze with viridian artists' oil paint tinted with a little French ultramarine and a tiny amount of yellow ocher. Apply liberally over the base coat.

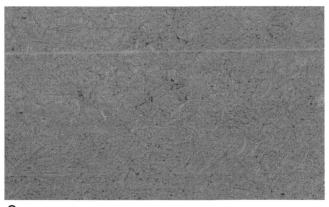

3 Stipple out brushstrokes to an even finish.

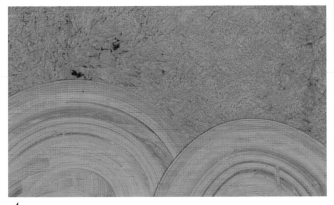

4 Tear a piece of thick cardboard along a straight edge, and pass this through the glaze in circular movements, butted against each other.

5 Continue over the entire base coat, creating a characteristically swirling malachite design.

6 Seal with two coats of gloss varnish for shine and protection.

Vinegar painting

1 Paint your chosen surface with two coats of eggshell paint in your preferred color.

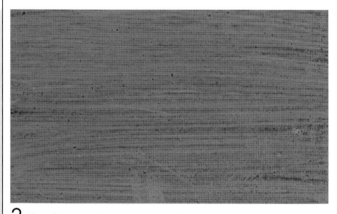

2 Mix the tinted vinegar paint from the recipe on page 188, and apply it to the base coat. Stipple away brushstrokes.

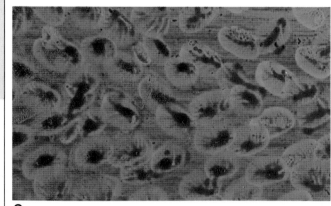

3 When the vinegar paint becomes tacky, form patterns on the surface with your chosen tool. Use bags, corks, crumpled paper – or just your finger. Allow to dry for up to seven days before varnishing.

Old pewter

1 Paint your surface with silver acrylic paint (use spray paint if you prefer). Allow to dry, and cover with a liberal coat of black acrylic paint.

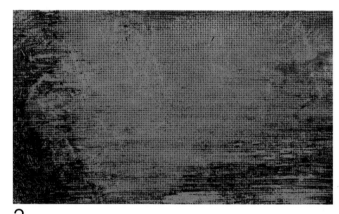

2 While the paint is still wet, wipe it over with a lint-free cloth to produce an aged and distressed look.

3 Add some stencilling – we chose old nuts and rivets – and a little yellow ocher and raw sienna to simulate rust. Allow to dry, and protect with appropriate varnish.

1 Paint your surface with two coats of pale yellow eggshell, thoroughly drying overnight between coats.

4 Carefully cross-drag with a dragging brush to emulate the look of the tortoiseshell.

2 Mix a gilp (see p.189), or use ready-made transparent oil glaze, and apply to the ground surface.

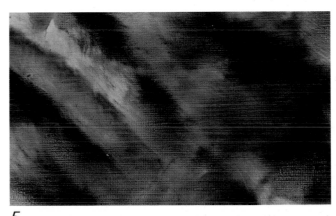

5 Apply a little black oil paint, and cross-drag again.

3 While the gilp (see p.189) is still wet, paint on small streaks of burnt umber, yellow ocher and burnt sienna oil paint, mixed with a little glaze.

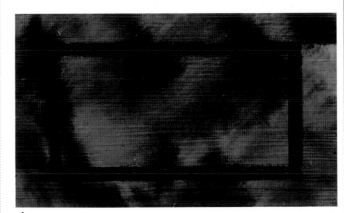

6 Speckle or spatter sparingly with a raw umber and black. Soften. Create a frame with tape and paint with black acrylic paint. Finally, protect with a coat of gloss varnish.

Stonewall

1 Paint the base coat in a magnolia vinyl semigloss (silk) latex (emulsion) and allow to dry.

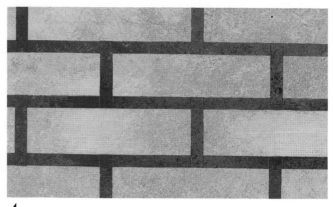

4 Mix another glaze of a very pale green-gray, and color wash again carefully accentuating the area on either side of the tape. This will show up the mortar.

2 Mark out stone slabs with chalk lines, and tape with low-tack masking tape to create "mortar."

5 Delicately spatter a little black and white in random positions over the wall. Use a small amount of ocher to paint haphazard fine cracks.

3 Mix an acrylic glaze with some yellow ocher paint, and color wash the entire wall quite randomly. Allow to dry.

6 Carefully remove the tape. Seal the wall with some acrylic varnish if it is particularly vulnerable. Add a stenciled design of leaves to the wall if desired.

1 Paint your surface with two coats of vinyl semigloss (silk) latex (emulsion) and allow to dry thoroughly.

2 Measure and cut out stencils of your design, keeping both positive and negative parts. The simpler the pattern, the better.

3 Cut out 1 in (2.5 cm) squares of foam (carpet padding), and fix each with strong glue to a piece of wood.

4 Attach the positive parts of your stencil to the wall with spray adhesive or low-tack masking tape. Load a foam square with your chosen acrylic color, and carefully print across the entire background.

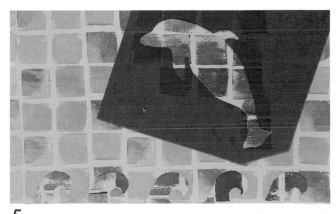

5 Change the positive for the negative image of your stencil, and paint the infill section with the foam squares.

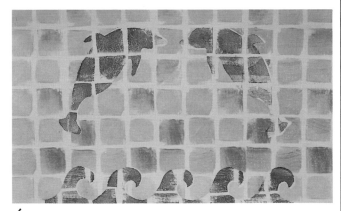

6 Remove the stencil, and allow to dry thoroughly before protecting with at least one coat of acrylic varnish.

Pushing Back the Boundaries

Initiative and experimentation are exciting, and can result in some marvelous effects. Although there are rules to observe when using both oil- and water-based paints, glazes, and varnishes, certain exceptions can be made. Oil and water do not mix, it is true, but this can be used to advantage. Try spattering, sponging, or spraying oil-based or water-based paint onto its opposite base coat while still wet. The separations caused, when allowed to dry, can yield some striking and satisfactory effects. You can also dab or spatter the wet surface with its own solvent. Combine wet spray paints, and use additives, such as fine (silver) sand, sawdust, or wood and plaster fillers, to create a range of exciting textures. Mix a little filler or plaster of Paris into the paint for a three-dimensional effect. If you make a mistake, and the result is pleasing, use it! It might not be right for the current project, but if it looks good, recreate it elsewhere; you never know, you may just have launched the next generation of decorating ideas!

Making your own materials

Making paints, glazes, and varnishes for the creation of your own unusual finishes is not as daunting as you might think. So long as you bear in mind the basic rules of use and protection for the differently based paints (see p.8–10), most ideas are possible. Here are some recipes for you to try.

Crackle Glaze

This can be bought ready-made to create the impression of cracked paint characteristic of weathered houses and antique furniture. Bought over the counter, as crackle glaze or peeling paint medium, it can be expensive. An excellent substitute is liquid gum arabic, available ready-mixed from art supply stores. Or you can buy it in crystalline form and dissolve it in boiling water to the consistency of cream. Use a ratio of 1 lb (½ kg) of crystals to 2–3 pt (1–1½ liters) of water. Store in an airtight jar. Kept at 41–95°F (5–35°C), it should remain usable for up to two years.

Two-part crackle glaze (known as craquelure) is used to create the fine spider's-web cracking seen on the surface of old oil paintings. This comes as a ready-made product in two parts: a base and a top coat. Create your own by utilizing a ground coat of gold size (obtainable from good art, craft, or decorating supply stores) with a top coat of liquid gum arabic (described above), adding a few drops of dishwashing detergent to act as a binder.

Tinted Varnishes

Use tinted varnishes either as an antique or a colored transparent finish.

Water-based Varnish

Tint water-based varnish with universal stainers, water-based artist's acrylic or gouache paints, or powder pigments. Dissolve a little of the color in the solvent first, and mix thoroughly. Add a small amount of the varnish to be tinted, and mix thoroughly again. Add the mixture to the full varnish quantity, and again blend thoroughly. This process eliminates "streaks" caused by the undissolved paint.

Oil-based Varnishes

Tint in the same way, with universal stainers, powder colors, or artist's oil paints.

LEFT A convincing tortoiseshell effect is given to a wood table. The same effect can be easily achieved on wall panels.
RIGHT Wood-grained panels make an ideal background to set off richly-colored antiques.

Paints

There are many suitable types of paint available over the counter (see Materials, pp.8–10). However, some more traditional paints can be mixed at home, and used with many decorating techniques. These include limewash, distemper, and true milk paints, along with simple homemade wash.

Distemper

This is an old-style paint, used for the painting of walls both interior and exterior. It allows the passage of moisture, and is therefore especially useful where a house has been plagued with dampness.

> ### INGREDIENTS FOR DISTEMPER
> 1 lb (½ kg) whiting
> ½ gallon (2.25 liters) water
> Gesso (see below)
> Stainers, powder pigment, or water-based acrylics
>
> ### METHOD
> Sift the whiting into the water, and allow to stand overnight. Discard about 1–2 in (2.5–5 cm) of the top clear water, and add about 10 percent of gesso. Stir thoroughly, and tint with universal stainers, powder pigments, or water-based artists' acrylics.

> ### Gesso
> ½ cup (4 oz/125 g) rabbit-skin glue powder
> 10 fl oz (285 ml) boiling water
> 9 oz (250 g) whiting
> Powder pigment (optional)
>
> ### METHOD
> Make the gesso in a double-boiler, or a container standing in hot water. Stir the water slowly into the glue powder. Sift in the whiting, and stir the mixture to a thick, creamy consistency. The gesso can be tinted with powder pigments. The most traditional are the earth colors – ocher, red, and terra cotta.

Limewash

This is another traditional and inexpensive paint, used in home decoration for thousands of years. It consists of "slaked" lime (lime mixed with water) and pigment. Limewash dries quickly to a characteristic flat and hard-wearing finish, and is well suited to interior walls, such as those in kitchens, bedrooms, and bathrooms. It can also be used for aged and "distressed" effects, created by removing some of the paint and allowing the base color to show through. The best way to achieve this is to wet a tough rag with denatured alcohol (methylated spirits), and rub it hard all over the surface. Always use gloves and protective clothes when working with this paint, and handle it with extreme care. Limewash should preferably be used on a permeable or porous surface, and not over modern latex (emulsion) paints, which seal the walls. If the surface has already been painted, sand it before applying the limewash.

> ### INGREDIENTS FOR LIMEWASH
> 8 oz (225 g) lime putty
> 1 gallon (4.5 liters) water
> Powder pigment
>
> ### METHOD
> Pour the water into a clean container, and slowly add about 8 oz (225 g) of lime. Stir gently but thoroughly to eliminate lumps. Be extremely careful during this entire process, because when the lime meets the water, a bubbling reaction will occur, allowing the emission of vapors which are not dangerous but should be avoided. When the reaction has stopped, stir again, adding more water until you obtain the consistency of thin cream. Dissolve the pigment in a little water and stir well. Add it to the limewash, while constantly stirring.

Vinegar Paint

Vinegar painting, or vinegar graining (see p.182) was a bold technique used mainly in the 19th century by American furniture craftsmen to create patterned effects on simple pieces of furniture. The effect is still applied today, using a mixture such as the one below.

> ### INGREDIENTS FOR VINEGAR PAINT
> Powder pigment of the chosen color
> 7 fl oz (200 ml) brown malt vinegar
> 1 tsp sugar
> Dishwashing detergent
>
> ### METHOD
> Mix the powder pigment to a thick creamy paste with 2–3 tablespoons of the vinegar. Pour in the remainder of the vinegar, and stir thoroughly. Add the sugar and a few drops of dishwashing detergent to act as a binder. Mix thoroughly once again, and store in an airtight container.

Milk Paint

Most of the milk paints available on the market today incorporate binders other than those made from milk protein, so as to prevent the paint from going rancid. They retain the characteristics of traditional milk paint without the harmful lime or lead content. You can achieve a completely authentic look by making your own simulated milk paint, but you must use it immediately, because it cannot be stored. Once applied, it dries in the air and will therefore not become rancid. Protect it only in a vulnerable area or on furniture, using a suitable varnish or furniture wax.

Latex (Emulsion) Glaze or Paint Wash

Pour your chosen latex (emulsion) paint or glaze straight from
the can into a large, clean container. Stir thoroughly to obtain
an even, lump-free consistency. Add water, stirring constantly,
to the strength required. Note the quantity of water used.
Proportions can vary from 1 part paint to 6–10 parts water. Mix
enough for your day's work. Repeat as necessary each day.

Simple Water-based Color Wash

INGREDIENTS
3–4 tbsp powder pigment
1¾ pt (1 liter) water
3–5 fl oz (100–150 ml) polyvinyl acetate (PVA)
medium or glue

METHOD
Mix your powder pigment with a little water to a
creamy consistency. Dilute the polyvinyl acetate medium or
glue with a little water, and add to the paint mixture
as a binder. Stir well. The amounts suggested here
should be enough to color wash
an average room.

Gilp

This is the liquid on which oil color is "floated" for techniques
such as marbling (see p.175) and tortoiseshelling (see p.183).
It is not available over the counter but can easily be made at
home when needed. The recipe is similar to that for glaze, but
does not contain whiting. Gilp is usually mixed just before use,
because it can separate, and does not store well.

INGREDIENTS FOR GILP
1 part pure turpentine
1 part boiled linseed oil
1/20 liquid driers

METHOD
Mix all of the ingredients together thoroughly and use as
soon as possible. Remember that the more driers you add,
the quicker the drying time, and therefore the shorter your
working time. If you do store the gilp, keep it in an airtight
glass container, and use it up within a few weeks.

*ABOVE A subtle marble paint
effect on the walls of this
dining room and hall creates
a light and airy, yet
sophisticated appearance.*

Index

190

Index

Credits

Elizabeth Whiting & Associates page 2, Tom Leighton page 8, Brian Harrison page 10, Jean Paul Bonhommet page 21 and page 189, Di Louis page 186, Huntley Hepworth page 187.

All other photographs are the copyright of Quarto Publishing plc.

Quarto Publishing plc would like to thank ICI Paints who kindly supplied the colors from their Colour Palette range for use in this book. For more information contact Dulux Advice Line, telephone number: 01753 550 555 International Code 44 + 1753.

Ray Bradshaw would like to give his thanks and gratitude to both Sally MacEachern and Toni Toma for their never-ending support and help during the production of this book. Their understanding and total committment certainly never faltered and for that he is eternally grateful.

Index by Dawn Butcher.